Natives, Newcomers, Exiles, Fugitives

Northern California Writers and Their Work

Natives,
Newcomers,
Exiles,
Fugitives

Northern California
Writers and Their Work

Jonah Raskin

Running Wolf Press
Healdsburg, California
2003

For Adam, Adelina, Ann, Dan and Fred

Library of Congress Control Number: 2003090425

Raskin, Jonah

Natives, Newcomers, Exiles, Fugitives:
Northern California Writers and Their Work/ Jonah Raskin

ISBN 0-9701333-8-3

1.   California – literature. 2. Regional literature – California.
3.   West coast writing and writers – California

Printed in the United States of America by Barlow Printing

Book design by Chip Wendt and Martha Dwyer
Cover art by Jack Stuppin

Portions of this book have appeared in slightly different form in
The Press Democrat, Santa Rosa, California.

Published by
Running Wolf Press
104 Matheson Street
Healdsburg, California 95448

*Running Wolf Press books may be ordered online from
the "Local Authors" page of Toyonbooks.com*

Acknowledgments

Many individuals helped to make this book possible – the authors whose books I reviewed and whom I profiled in the pages of *The Press Democrat*. I want to thank my editors at *The Press Democrat* – Pete Golis, Patty Hayes and Richard Nelson. I also want to thank the *PD* for permission to reprint these reviews and interviews. I'm indebted to the many readers who have written or spoken to me about my reviews and interviews. A special thanks to Dorianne Laux and The Permissions Company for permission to quote from her poem, "What Could Happen." Publicity people at publishing companies and at bookstores helped to arrange for interviews and to provide me with review copies, often in the nick of time. I'm especially grateful to Jane Love at Copperfield's Books. I want to thank Martha Dwyer and Chip Wendt at Running Wolf Press, Jack Stuppin for his art on the cover of this book, and Jack Ritchie at the Jean and Charles Schulz Information Center at Sonoma State University for help with research. My colleagues in the Communication Studies Department were always supportive, especially Cathy Stuckey, Benét Leigh and Melinda Barnard. Karen Petersen provided suggestions for the reading list. J.J. Wilson was consistently encouraging – an inspiring reader and critic. I also want to extend my appreciation to Robin Pressman at KRCB radio, Carolina Clare at North Light Books and Naomi Schneider at the University of California Press. Gerald Haslam has taught me a lot about California life and letters. Other teachers include Hector Lee, Bob Coleman, Tillie Olsen, and James Houston.

Contents

Part III: Private Eyes

Part IV: Voyagers, Visionaries, Historians

Part V: Women Warriors

Appendix

Natives, Newcomers, Exiles, Fugitives

The hills
Rise above the town, nudge houses and shops
Toward the valley, kick the shallow river
Into place.

– Dorianne Laux
"What Could Happen"

Introduction

❄

Over the past several decades, northern California has changed dramatically. So has the literary scene. Now there *is* a literary scene, and more than that, a literary culture. Now there are writers everywhere you turn – from Petaluma to Petrolia, St. Helena to San Rafael. Now there's renewed interest in the literary past and in our literary ancestors – Jack London and M.F.K. Fisher. There are hundreds of writers in northern California and each one of them is unique. Still, they have all been shaped in one way or another by the region – by its history, geography and culture, and in turn they have all helped to shape and define the region. Our writers have held up a mirror in which we have been able to see ourselves and the world in which we live. They show us as fragile and yet resilient, lost and yet very much at home. The male writers tend to be wild men; the women are often warriors of one sort or another. Our writers, like writers all over the state, explore the California dream and the California nightmare. And then, too, we have our share of mystery writers and authors of detective fiction.

Natives, Newcomers, Exiles, Fugitives is meant to be a lively and provocative contribution to the on-going northern California debate about the local literary world. From my point of view, we have a rich and diverse culture. I have never been comfortable – though I have certainly tried to be – with the views of Dana Gioia, the Sonoma County poet, critic and Bush appointee to the Chairmanship of the National Endowment for the Arts. Gioia has argued that the quality of northern California literature has declined since 1900, that there is no cultural center here and no significant literary publications. I do not believe in progress in the arts, and to rate the writers of the present with the writers of the past – as though they had some intrinsic value – does not seem like a fruitful exercise. I do believe that there are many innovative and creative writers at work today in this region and that there are high standards in literary journalism and cultural criticism. Gioia himself – the author of *Can Poetry Matter?* – is a case in point. Granted, there is no major literary center, but there are writers clustered all over northern California. There are new voices. There is experimentation and there are many individual talents who are reworking literary tradition. T.S. Eliot once said that there is a provincialism of time and a provincialism of place. Northern California is no longer immune to the cross currents of American cultural life, and northern California writers are certainly aware of the rich literary past of this region. This is a time of ferment and growth.

When I first arrived from New York in 1975, our writers seemed few and far between. Author appearances in local bookstores were rare events indeed. Folks ventured forth to see the prize pigs, sheep and cows that the 4-H kids nurtured – they were worth seeing – and for pancake breakfasts to raise money for local fire departments. The fairs and the fundraisers still go on, but now there's a book culture to go along with the agriculture.

The first book party I attended took place at the Bodega Fire Department, not far from the Pacific Ocean. There was a good turnout that day for Chester Aaron – who was born in Pennsylvania – but as a rule folks did not come out to see writers, and in those days writers didn't seem to care that much about being seen and heard either. The idea of "literature" was suspect in some circles – even in academic circles – but it was also beloved, especially among farmers and ranchers, many of them European immigrants who would rather read Tolstoi and Thomas Mann than watch TV.

If I wanted serious writers, I was often told, I had best look elsewhere. Why didn't I go back to New York? More than one neighbor asked me that question. I have remained here, perversely perhaps, and I have kept looking for writers, though at times I have thought that I might be looking in the wrong place. Henry James – who thought a lot about the connections between literature and society – once said that for literature to thrive it was essential to have a rich cultural soil and solid institutions. I've wrestled with that idea for years, and I've come to the conclusion that James was right. Literary geniuses like Jack London and M.F.K. Fisher seem able to thrive anywhere, but most of us need community, cultural roots and a sense of history. And roots, history and community take time, as Henry James understood.

The longer I have lived here, the more writers I have met and grown to admire. The literary community has grown, cultural traditions have become richer and more complex, and as a literary environment we've developed a keen appreciation of the past. Like me, many writers have come from other towns and other cities all across America. Soon after I arrived, I met J. J. Wilson – who came from Virginia – and Karen Petersen, a native who was born and raised in Petaluma. Together Wilson and Petersen wrote about unknown women artists from around the world, and their work inspired local women artists. I met Bill Barich who was from Long Island and who wrote about horse racing and fishing for the *New Yorker* no less. There was Jerry Rosen who came from the Bronx and wrote about his family in the Bronx. There was Gaye LeBaron, *The Press Democrat's* premier columnist, who wrote authoritatively about local history, and Professor Hector Lee who rewrote the lore of northern California's heroes and villains. The list grew larger and larger: Jim Dodge, Dana Gioia, Joy Sterling, Mavis Jukes.

The local scene experienced setbacks as well as advances. There was no steady line of literary development. At times, I felt I'd never find a lasting literary scene. Then a new wave of writers would suddenly break on these shores – even writers like Chile's Isabel Allende – who came from distant continents and who felt like exiles.

Increasingly, too, men and women who had been born and raised in northern California began to write fiction about this place and its people. The insiders had advantages the interlopers and outsiders didn't have, especially if they had listened to tales about the secret past. Greg Sarris makes his home in Los Angeles and teaches at UCLA, but he grew up in Santa Rosa among Native Americans. In *Grand Avenue* and *Watermelon Nights* he tells the hidden history and mythology of our region. Sarris is the closest thing we have to William Faulkner – a novelist who makes our own little world into a whole universe.

In the mid-1980s, I started a summer writers' conference at Sonoma State University. Suzanne Lipsett was a spark plug. Gerald Haslam made an appearance, and Bill Barich paid a visit. Amy Tan – who had grown up in Santa Rosa – gave a talk, though no one paid that much attention. She hadn't yet published *The Joy Luck Club*, her first book, and she hadn't been discovered by the literary world at large. When I gave up the reins of the writers' conference, Robin Beeman took over. In addition to working on her own stories, Beeman taught writing at the Sitting Room, the community library in Cotati that has mostly served women, and that features women writers, both local and global.

Cultural institutions, like the Sitting Room, have sprung up all over

northern California, and so have publications, like "The Reader's Rejoin-
der," a newsletter that the poet Don Emblen founded, edited and wrote for
when he wasn't printing chapbooks and broadsides at The Clamshell
Press. Today, Susan Bono publishes fiction and non-fiction in "Tiny
Lights," Barbara Baer operates *Floreant Press*, and Chip Wendt publishes
poems and stories at *Running Wolf Press*.

In the mid-1980s, I began to write book reviews and profiles of
local authors. For years I worked with Rich Nelson, the book editor at *The
Press Democrat*, and Nelson encouraged me to take risks and challenge
readers' assumptions and expectations. When he departed for San Diego, I
worked with Patty Hayes, who kept an eye out for little known books by
local authors – like Charles Rubin, another ex-New Yorker – eager for and
deserving of attention.

I had published book reviews in *The San Francisco Chronicle*
when William Hogan was the editor – and later when Pat Holt and Alex
Madrigal ran the show – but writing for *The Press Democrat* was different.
I liked being a local critic accountable to my neighbors and not to the
publicity department of a major publisher in Manhattan. As far as Manhattan was concerned, I was invisible. I enjoyed that invisibility; it gave me a
license to speak my mind.

The Sunday book pages of *The Press Democrat* have helped to
create a book culture in northen California. Sara Peyton and Victoria
McMains shared space with me at the *PD* and gave the book pages depth
and diversity. Librarians joined the burgeoning book culture, too, and the
bookstores played a part by holding author events, and making it possible
for readers and writers to meet, mix and talk. At North Light Books in
Cotati, Carolina Clare persuaded Guerneville's Dorothy Allison, the
reclusive author of *Bastard Out of Carolina*, to read from her work – a rare
treat indeed. At Copperfield's Books, Paul Jaffe, Jane Love and Tom
Montan lured famous writers here, like Anne Lamott, and encouraged the
growth of book clubs where friends would gather to talk about books –
and about babies, recipes, marriages and divorces.

Northern California's book culture has grown as the region as a
whole has grown; it has thrived as newcomers have collided with old
timers, and as the spirit of innovation has clashed with the weight of
tradition. Our literature has grown as wineries have grown, as creative
chefs have transformed our menus and our pallets, and as first-rate creative

writing teachers and creative writers themselves – Sherril Jaffe, Gillian Conoley, Noelle Oxenhandler – have come to Sonoma State University.

Over the past 30 years or so, northern California has lost much of its invisibility and anonymity. It isn't a literary backwater anymore. Now it's a destination for tourists as well as for authors on book tours. We belong on the literary map of America. We have come of age as a region for readers and for writers.

Part I:
Calls of the Wild

Jack London

Call of the Wild,
White Fang, & To Build a Fire

The Valley of the Moon
Introduction by Kevin Starr

Jack London's Golden State
Edited by Gerald Haslam

Jack London was the most popular, as well as the highest-paid, American author near the beginning of this century. Soon after his death at the age of 40, however, he was dislodged from his exalted position as top literary dog by younger talents like Ernest Hemingway and F. Scott Fitzgerald. For much of the 20th century, London has been far more admired in far-off places – like the Soviet Union – than in the United States. Today, he is largely unread and untaught in American high schools and colleges, and often ignored by the reading public at large. The prophet is indeed unappreciated at home, even in northern California where he was born and raised – perhaps because his passion for socialism, and his belief in the racial superiority of the white race seem muddle-headed and embarrassing in a culture that demands that popular writers be politically correct.

London's current status on the fringe of literary respectability seems to be changing once again. There's a new wonderful Jack London web site that is edited by SSU Professor Clarice Stasz, who is also the author of *American Dreamers: Charmian and Jack London*. There are also three new books that make London's work more accessible. The first volume is a collection of classic tales from the "Northland" – *The Call of the Wild, White Fang,* and *To Build a Fire –* which Modern Library included in its list of the 100 best novels of the 20th century (London was number 88, a long way behind James Joyce, William Faulkner and D.H. Lawrence). The second volume is *The Valley of the Moon*, an epic novel from 1913 that was originally serialized in *Cosmopolitan Magazine* before the magazine fell entirely to the "Cosmo Girl." The third volume is *Jack London's Golden State*, a compendium of fiction and non-fiction, edited and with an introduction and a bibliography by Gerald Haslam. Reading these books you appreciate London not only as a progenitor of California literature, but as a creative genius who had the ability to turn his own protean life into the stuff of myth and legend. While his flaws are apparent in these three books, so are his strengths for telling dramatic tales with primal themes.

The Call of the Wild, *White Fang*, and *To Light a Fire* are the three works of London's that are most often associated with his name, and fans at home and abroad will have no trouble remembering them. To those who have never read London, the Modern Library volume is the most logical place to begin. *The Call of the Wild* and *White Fang* are, as London himself explained, companion pieces, each one the "antithesis" of the other. Both stories resound with breathtaking poetry and thought-provoking philosophy, and both stories are, of course, about the nature of human beings, including the complex being named Jack London, as well as about two polar-opposite canines.

In case you haven't read the stories or don't remember them, let me say this: Buck, the protagonist in *The Call of the Wild*, is a domesticated dog from "the sun-kissed Santa Clara Valley" who reverts to his feral past in the frozen Yukon. White Fang is a wolf-dog from the Yukon who becomes tamed by "human kindness" in the "Southland." While these stories reflect the ideas and the values of pernicious social Darwinism they also resonate with raw power and a sense of aesthetic beauty. I don't think that anyone who has ever read them is quite the same again.

The Valley of the Moon, London's 1913 novel, is set entirely in northern California. It begins in Oakland and ends in the Sonoma Valley, and it takes place sometime between the 1906 earthquake and the outbreak of World War I. It's a swan song of sorts by a man disillusioned with socialism who is searching for a new way of life and new ideals. The University of California Press has publicized it as "a road novel fifty years before Kerouac," hoping perhaps to ride the current popularity of books by Beat Generation authors. *The Valley of the Moon* does include a hefty section in which the two main characters, Billy and Saxon, travel around northern California, but this is hardly a road novel in the current sense of the term. Unlike the Beats, Billy and Saxon walk on their own two feet.

They never travel by car, bus or train. Unlike the Beats, they want to settle down, sink roots, grow vegetables and raise horses, not go as fast as they can in search of existential adventure for its own sake. Billy and Saxon are hard-working refugees from the working class; they're more akin to the upwardly mobile characters in a Horatio Alger story than to the crazy hipsters in *On the Road.*

Part of the charm of the novel is provided by the details of living in northern California nearly 100 years ago. In Oakland, Billy and Saxon go to the "moving picture show" for entertainment. In Carmel, they harvest mussels and abalone and frolic with bohemians. In Sonoma County they buy 20 acres for $50 an acre (what a deal!) and set about raising horses and chickens, cultivating berries, making jams and having fun. I'm tempted to describe them as hybrid creatures somewhere between hippies and yuppies but that may be stretching the point.

Throughout the text there's an annoying litany of complaints about the newer immigrants from southern Europe who are supplanting the old Anglo-Saxon settlers. In his introduction to *The Valley of the Moon,* California State Librarian Kevin Starr doesn't overlook the novel's "strong racist overtones," but he also argues that despite "its flaws and inconsistencies," it appeals to "that dream of a better life which many call California." I would agree. As a refugee from the political turmoil of the 1960s who settled in Sonoma County in the 1970s, I identify with Billy and with Saxon. In fact, I'll take the bright, green richness of the countryside here over the sprawling, smudged cities of the Bay Area almost any day of the year.

Jack London's Golden State, which is deftly edited by Gerald Haslam, offers brief, tantalizing selections from the novels, including *The Sea-Wolf, Martin Eden,* and *The Iron Heel,* a futuristic fable about a brutal oligarchy and the rebel underground in America, that influenced George Orwell when he sat down to write *Nineteen Eighty-Four.* There's also a delightful autobiographical essay that London wrote at age 30 in which he described his own haunting loneliness, his days on both sides of the law, and his reading and writing. Though he doesn't describe his own birth outside of wedlock, which obviously shaped his feral orphan personality, he's candid about his habits and feelings. "I am not only careless and irregular, but melancholy," he noted insightfully about himself.

Haslam provides brief introductions to the individual selections and an introductory essay about London, whom he describes as a "literary outsider." Indeed, it is in large part London's status as an outsider, and his role as a spokesman for other outsiders, that makes him so appealing, and that ensures that the call of Jack London will continue to reverberate. I guess I wouldn't want him to be too readily or too easily accepted by the mainstream. Perhaps the prophet ought not to be wholeheartedly appreciated in his own country.

A Tale of Two Readers: Kevin Starr and Gerald Haslam

Kevin Starr, the California State Librarian, has surely read as much London as anyone else on the planet, and that's saying a lot since London wrote more than 50 books by the time he died in 1916 at the age of 40. Starr managed to get through his childhood and adolescence without reading a single book by London. "I didn't discover him until I was a graduate student at Harvard in the 1960s," he explains during a recent phone interview. "Then I soaked myself totally in London. I read everything he ever wrote and became mesmerized."

Starr has been monitoring the rise and fall of London's popularity over the course of the 20th century, and he suggests that while he has a cult-like status today among readers who offer total adulation, he has never been given the wider, fuller recognition in our culture that he genuinely deserves. "London ought to be in the same rank as Norris and Dreiser," Starr says. And he adds, "There is a protean talent to his engagement. He was a naturalist and an existentialist; he revealed the elemental life of human beings." Starr also feels that London will continue to be rediscovered and revisited by successive generations of readers. "London occupies a major place in California literature," he says. "A great many people learn about the state by reading London' s work. They see the Golden State through his eyes."

Gerald Haslam, the editor of *Jack London's Golden State*, read *Call of the Wild* when he was still in high school, and he has gone on reading and rereading him ever since. He has also taught London at Sonoma State University, and has introduced several generations of students to his fiction and non-fiction. "I've noticed that London's work is missing from a lot of recent anthologies of American literature," Haslam says ruefully. "He is overlooked today. He's outré from the point of view of a great many New York critics." Like Starr, Haslam has monitored the rise and fall of London's popularity and he observes that "he comes in and out of vogue."

Like many readers, Haslam himself prefers London's short stories to his novels. Get him going on the subject and he becomes passionate about "The Apostate," a brilliant fable about a "perfect worker" who becomes a "perfect machine" and descends the ladder of evolution until he turns into a "sickly ape." Haslam regards London as a prototype of the American author. "Like many others who came after him, he tried to synthesize two diverse instincts," he explains. "London wanted to be both a tough guy and an intellectual and he never got it squared away."

Like Starr, Haslam doesn't idealize London, and like Starr he also admires him tremendously. "He never fully realized the full dimensions of his talent," Haslam says. "Still, he's one of the truly great talents that America has produced."

Gary Snyder

The Gary Snyder Reader:
Prose, Poetry, and Translations 1952-1998

Since the 1960s, Gary Snyder has been an icon of the environmental movement, and like most icons whether living or dead, he elicits two emphatic responses. On the one hand there's the inclination to worship at the Snyder altar. On the other hand there's the urge to engage in icon demolition.

Jim Dodge – the celebrated author of the contemporary folktale, *Fup* – is more silly than serious in his introduction to *The Gary Snyder Reader*, a monumental selection from nearly 50 years of Snyder's work. Identifying himself as "The Secretary of Foolishness in the Gary Snyder Appreciation Society," Dodge talks nearly as much about himself as about Snyder, and since they've been friends for years that is understandable. Still, the flippant tone is annoying. A sober, in-depth perspective on Snyder who is still going strong as a teacher at UC Davis, a writer, a public speaker, a sage and an eco-warrior, will have to wait until he is no longer a looming presence on the literary and environmental scene.

Snyder himself doesn't elicit wishy-washy responses to his controversial ideas about watersheds, logging, bio-regionalism, globalism or the need for compatibility between wilderness and civilization. On the contrary, he demands unflinching debate about the issues he raises and about his entire body of work, and hopefully that's what he'll get with the publication of *The Gary Snyder Reader*. What follows are my responses to Snyder's work – his essays, journals, poems, translations, letters and travel pieces – and a few tentative reflections about Snyder himself and his place in history.

Usually, part of the pleasure of reading essays derives from watching writers discover what they want to say in the process of writing. Snyder gives the impression that he knows exactly what he is going to say before he says it. He offers a thesis statement, defines his terms and moves systematically point by point. Unfortunately there's little sense of play and almost no disclosure about his internal process.

Snyder is notorious for refusing to let outsiders into his emotional mandala, and the brief journal entries here reinforce his reputation as a strict guardian of his own privacy. We don't learn about his parents, his marriages, his children or his pivotal relationships with his Reed College classmates. Now and then, he lifts the curtain and reveals a corner of his own mind. "If one wished to write poetry of nature, where an audience?" he wrote in 1952. That question reverberated for years. After a lot of travel and meditation, and a period in which he gave up on poetry, Snyder not only created his own audience, but a public persona for himself as a Zen Buddhist nature poet and a manly kind of poetry that fuses the everyday with the mythic. No wonder he won the Pulitzer Prize for poetry in 1975.

Snyder writes beautifully about the wilderness and about wild animals, and he invites readers to rethink their ideas about wildlife. He gazes down and examines the ground under his own feet, and he also looks above his head at the cosmos. There's a sense of magic and mystery in his work – a raw engagement with the naked universe – and there's also the saving grace of humor in many of the poems. Snyder has called himself "a naturalist of my own species," and one can appreciate the aptness of that remark in "Four Poems for Robin," "Changing Diapers," "Bubba Creek Haircut" and the Snyder classic, "I Went into the Maverick Bar," which describes a hippie/redneck encounter that took place in Farmington, New Mexico but that might have happened anywhere west of the Mississippi.

I don't know Chinese or Japanese and can't offer an expert opinion about Snyder's translations into English of the poetry of Miyazawa Kenji or Han-shan, but I like the spiritual feeling and the sense of emotional urgency that he conveys. Snyder seems to respect the original – both the language and the culture – and at the same time he manages to transport Asian poetical traditions into a contemporary American idiom.

Snyder makes provocative comments in the two exuberant interviews that are reprinted in the book. "If there is any one thing that's unhealthy in America, it's that it's a whole civilization trying to get out of work," he told interviewer Peter Barry Chowka. If Snyder is often single-minded and inflexible, in the interviews there's dialogue and spontaneity, and occasionally he relaxes enough to talk about growing up in rural Washington, reading D.H. Lawrence, discovering Chinese art and the disciplined life in a Zen monastery in Japan. I'd begin this book with either the Chowka interview from *East West Journal* or the Eliot Weinberger interview which originally appeared in *The Paris Review*.

Snyder was never fit to be a tourist, and his accounts of passing through Australia and Zimbabwe are thin, but there are delightful accounts of traveling as a dharma bum to, and then across, the Indian subcontinent in the 1960s, long before spiritual pilgrimages were the thing to do in countercultural circles.

The section of letters is far too short, though now and then there's a radiant observation. In September 1955, for example, on the eve of Allen Ginsberg's historic reading of "Howl" in San Francisco, Snyder wrote prophetically to his friend Philip Whalen, "I think it will be a poetickall bombshell." American poetry hasn't been the same since that occasion, as Snyder suggests.

When I look back at Snyder's career, it seems to me that it took him years to recover from Jack Kerouac's celebration of him in *The Dharma Bums*. In that 1958 novel, which followed hard on the heels of *On the Road*, he appears as Japhy Ryder, "the great new hero of American culture." Snyder was only 28 at the time, largely unknown and largely unpublished. It's not surprising that after Kerouac's adulation he spent the next decade or so lying low in the Far East. It wasn't until the late 1960s that he settled in the Sierras.

Years ago, California Governor and now Oakland Mayor Jerry Brown told Snyder, "You're going against the grain of things all the time, aren't you?" (Brown also appointed Snyder to the Board of the California Arts Council, a position he held for six years.) Snyder has insisted that going against the grain is deeply ingrained in the human species. With the Beats and others, including protesters from the 1960s, he's revived a tradition of dissent and nonconformity that includes Anarchists, Luddites, Quakers, Wobblies, and Anabaptists, and that has taken moral courage – from the McCarthy days of the Cold War to the Reagan era of neo-conservatism.

In *The Paris Review* interview, Snyder says, "doom scenarios, even though they might be true, are not politically or psychologically effective." I think he's forgetting that the Ban the Bomb movement of the 1950s and 1960s, and the anti-nuclear power movement of the 1980s, were both built in part on doom scenarios about nuclear holocaust and nuclear meltdowns that mobilized millions of citizens around the world.

In the *East West* interview with Chowka, Snyder wisely observes that "there's no quiet place in the woods where you can take it easy and be a stoned-out hippie." But Snyder himself helped to fuel the hippie phenomenon by his own lifestyle and writing. In "Buddhism and the Coming Revolution," a seminal essay from the late 1960s that isn't included here, perhaps because it's too embarrassing now, Snyder wrote, "If we are lucky we may eventually arrive at a totally integrated world culture with matrilineal descent, free-form marriage, natural-credit communist economy, less industry, far less population and lots more national parks."

Of course, Snyder isn't the only rebel from that heady time to indulge in utopian poppycock. What makes him unusual is that he has continued his journey of spiritual exploration and political protest decade after decade. There are a great many ideas – about enlightenment and freedom, artistic genius and religious ecstasy, to name just a few – that are worth considering in these pages. *The Gary Snyder Reader* provides the opportunity to dig into a rich and complex body of work, try out the ideas, and dispense with the icon altogether.

Gary Snyder: The View from His Neck of the Woods

You don't have to talk to Gary Snyder for long to know which side he's on in the global and local battle that is waged everyday about the environment. "It's a lovely day here, and probably all over California," he says at the start of our phone conversation – as though he can actually see across the state from his niche in the Sierra Nevada. What Snyder mostly sees these days doesn't sound encouraging for environmentalists. In an instant he's all fired up about the fate of the Yuba River, the prognosis for farming, and the future of the forests in his neck of the woods.

"I'm on the northern boundary of Nevada County," he explains. "You have to cross the north fork of the Yuba River to get here. It's isolated and rural, and the population hasn't changed tremendously in the last 30 years, but the area is being rapidly developed now. We have subdivisions, and we have sprawl – suburban and wildlife-interface sprawl. There has been loss of farmland, and ordinary people have been pitted against relentless builders, contractors and developers who don't want to let go of a cash cow."

From Snyder's point of view, the story of California from the very beginning, and especially since the discovery of gold in 1849, has been a story of unremitting human greed. What's more he seems to take it personally – as though it's his space that's been defiled. "It's very unfortunate," he says. "Early on there was the draining of wetlands, the coming of the railroads, and the development of a corporate style of agriculture. California has always been a land of high-rollers and corrupt politicians."

But true to form, Snyder doesn't despair. In his own community, and in his own extended backyard he sees positive changes that he attributes to 20 years of steady environmental activism. "Four out of our five county supervisors are intelligent," he says. "They understand that we have to control growth, protect water, preserve habitat. There's a move here to declare the Yuba River a wild and scenic river, and there's opposition because people are afraid that the movement might spread, and that other communities might want to protect their wild and scenic rivers."

Meanwhile, Snyder is doing his best to protect and to maintain his own patch of the universe. Outside, there's manzanita that has to be cleared and a truck to be repaired. Inside, the library needs to be thinned-out. "I cut my own firewood," he says. "I take care of the forest and I farm and garden. I have the best tools – shovels, axes, saws – and I take very good care of them."

For years Snyder has been fond of saying that since the age of 17 or so, he's never done anything he hasn't wanted to do. More than any other comment, this one arouses my curiosity. When I ask him to explain, he says, "Some of the choices I've made have been hard, but I've always pursued what I have really wanted to do. I've never backed away from whatever life has offered me."

When I ask Snyder to explain how he and his contemporaries in the 1940s stack up against students today, he shows an unexpected side of himself. "There was a hopelessness about the Cold War," he says. "But at least we could define the enemy – Stalinism in Russia, the military in this country – and we began to look for alternatives. Today it's harder to say who the bad guys are, and harder to identify the alternatives. You can't stop globalism, but how do you temper it?" Snyder doesn't seem to have ready-made answers, though he does have lots of questions and suggestions, too. "Maybe we need to build up in already existing cities, rather than out into rural areas," he says.

The Beats were, of course, one of the alternatives to the culture of the Cold War, and Snyder remembers, as though it were yesterday, the legendary 1955 poetry reading at the Six Gallery in San Francisco that kicked off the Beat movement. "That event launched all of us," he says. "It launched Allen Ginsberg, of course, and Phil Whalen, and Michael McClure, and Jack Kerouac. After the Six Gallery, poetry readings became regular cultural events not only in this country, but all over the world."

Jim Dodge

Not Fade Away

The fantastic and the matter-of-fact coexist in *Fup,* Jim Dodge's best-selling New Age fable about a mallard duck, a wild pig and a gargantuan young man named Tiny. They coexist again in his novel, *Not Fade Away*, a wild paean to rock 'n' roll, the freedom of the open road, and the powers of the unfettered imagination.

Fup was set in the rainy coastal hills of northern California, Dodge's own stomping grounds. *Not Fade Away* begins in the same locale. A backwoodsman – with an uncanny resemblance to the author himself – smashes his truck, and wanders in a daze until he is rescued by George Gastin. Like Coleridge's ancient mariner, Gastin has a strange tale he is compelled to tell, a tale as tall as the redwoods that tower above him.

Gastin takes us back to the raucous days of his youth in the late 1950s and early 1960s, a legendary era that has been celebrated in nostalgic films like George Lucas's *American Graffiti* and Francis Ford Coppola's *Peggy Sue Got Married.* As the main character and the chief narrator, Gastin is part man, part myth. In San Francisco's North Beach he carouses with the Beats – Jack Kerouac and Neal Cassady – and in affluent neighborhoods he steals deluxe cars, destroys them and splits the insurance money with his criminal cohort, Scumball Johnson. Unlike Scumball, Gastin is a good-hearted con artist, not a hardened ex-con, and he's offered a chance to redeem himself when a white Cadillac El Dorado, license plate BOP 333, falls into his hands. The vintage Caddy is a gift from a wealthy woman to J.P. Richardson, aka the Big Bopper of "Chantilly Lace" fame. It's not a problem that the woman is dead, and no problem, either, that Richardson is dead, too, a victim of a plane crash that claimed the lives of rock immortals Buddy Holly and Ritchie Valens.

Gastin plans to drive the car all the way to Richardson's grave. On the road – pursued by both the police and thieves and haunted by his own demons – he has an "adventure in consciousness" that transforms his sorry life. There isn't much sex, but there's an abundance of drugs and of course tons of rock 'n' roll. Gastin plays golden oldies on an ear-popping sound system as he burns up the highways. The hits keep coming, from "La Bamba" and "Donna" to "Great Balls of Fire" and "Like a Rolling Stone."

Dodge follows the literary road that the Beats, the Merry Pranksters and Hunter S. Thompson have paved. He borrows, too, from French surrealism. But *Not Fade Away* is no repeat performance. Dodge dips into his own bag of magical tricks and dispenses his unique style of slapstick humor and homespun philosophy that made *Fup* endearing. There are puns aplenty, word play on every page, and the metaphors pile up higher and higher until the white Cadillac becomes almost as big and ominous a symbol as Herman Melville's white whale. Dodge keeps the literary pedal to the metal, and pushes language to the limit.

The San Francisco section of *Not Fade Away* is the least inspired, though it plays a necessary part, giving the story the down-to-earth quality it needs. In Arizona, Texas and Nebraska, Dodge plunges into wild states of mind. Cacti dance in the desert and little orange men crawl out of the woodwork. On the way to the Big Bopper's grave, Gastin slows down long enough to pick up a series of bizarre hitchhikers.

Double-Gone Johnson – a black minister and founder of the Rock Solid Gospel Light Church – crowns Gastin with a hat the color of pink flamingoes, and preaches a sweet sermon about rock, jazz, spirituals and the blues. Phillip Lewis Kerr hands Gastin a business card that boasts, "Greatest Traveling Salesman in the World," and promptly makes good on his claim by persuading Gastin to buy his own ghost.

On Halloween, Gastin's ghost joins him in the front seat of the Cadillac. Together they tune in to Captain Midnight, KRZE's cosmic disc jockey, and listen to monologues by the likes of Christopher Columbus, John Henry and the multi-millionaire J.P. Morgan. Gastin's surreal voyage into the chaos of the American night carries him into the heart of our deepest, darkest landscape.

Dodge has a sharp ear for the sounds of American speech, and reading his novel often feels like listening to a free-form radio station that can't help but blast away at everything that's safe and secure.

Rock 'n' roll did just that to the safe, sanitized Eisenhower era in the 1950s. Dodge's *Not Fade Away* celebrates the music that delivered us from the days of old. "Hail, hail rock 'n' roll," Chuck Berry sang. Dodge adds his voice to Berry's – to Buddy Holly's and J.P. Richardson's. Like their music, his novel shakes, rattles and rolls.

Jim Dodge: Driving Down Memory Lane

It's a cloudless Monday morning and Jim Dodge is listening to the Talking Heads on his tape deck as he drives down Memory Lane. More than 20 years ago, he came here on Saturday nights to cruise with the guys, listen to rock 'n' roll, and check out the action on the street. Here might be almost anywhere in America, but for Dodge it's Mendocino Avenue in downtown Santa Rosa.

A lot of Santa Rosans still remember Dodge. He was the clean-cut kid in the '51 Ford, the razzle-dazzle half-back on the Montgomery High School football team who took Chuck Berry as seriously as he took science and math. Now he's a local hero with a continental reputation, thanks to the popularity of *Fup* and *Not Fade Away*.

"I had a peripatetic childhood," Dodge says. "Every six months my father packed his bags and moved us to another air force base. The back seat of a car was where I grew up."

Still, for all their continental travels, the Dodge family always returned to Santa Rosa, and Dodge lived in town long enough to make friends and be elected senior class president at Montgomery High School. After graduation from Montgomery, he attended Humboldt State and began to study fisheries management. Then the 1960s blew into town and Dodge's plans changed.

"Revolution was in the air," he says. "We had madcap dreams. We liked to go fast and very close to the edge. We believed that reality was what we perceived it to be, and that we could change it."

Dodge changed his major and moved to Iowa, where he studied creative writing. For the holidays, he always drove home and on the way he had strange experiences. "I can remember riding in my '59 Ford, listening to Bob Dylan's 'Desolation Row' on the radio and feeling utter desolation," he says.

When he sat down to write *Not Fade Away*, those memories came back to him. "I wanted *Not Fade Away* to end in a place of desolation," Dodge says. "Like Job in the Old Testament, Gastin has sought the answers to all the big questions about good and evil, God and the devil, heaven and hell. No message is received. Gastin is torn between acceptance and doubt, affirmation and negation. But he also knows that there is beauty in desolation, and that desolation can give birth to hope."

When the 1960s skidded to a stop, Dodge's life took a dramatic turn. In 1970, he moved to the remote hills of Cazadero in western Sonoma County, where he planted trees, mended fences and healed some of the fissures in his own soul.

"I went from life in the fast lane, to near-total isolation," he says. "For several years I rarely left the ranch, and on the ranch, time slowed down."

Dodge and his friends at the Root Hog Ranch didn't have a single power tool. They did everything by hand. Dodge liked the simple life, the isolated existence. Over the years, he cultivated a habit of introspection and a keen awareness of place.

"I came to think of myself as a regional writer," he says. "The rain and the fog had a profound influence on my imagination. There's a certain Russian grimness on the coast, a sense of vast spaces that are cold, harsh, forbidding. The land began to dominate my consciousness."

In the rugged Cazadero terrain, Dodge found a territory conducive to the writing of *Fup*, his folk tale that bears a striking resemblance to the Russian story *Peter and the Wolf*.

After the publication of *Fup,* fame knocked on Dodge's front door. Ed Asner touted the tale as a panacea for the ills of the troubled soul and the sickness of society. *People* magazine published Dodge's photo and made his name a household word for a brief moment in history. All that media attention put Dodge's sense of identity to the ultimate test. Fortunately he had the friendship and support of Gary Snyder. "Gary took me under his wing," Dodge says. "He showed me how to survive the media crush, the demands, the dislocation." Dodge had met Snyder a decade earlier and they discovered that they had many of the same interests. "We've hiked but, oddly enough, never went backpacking," Dodge says. "It's a delight to travel with Gary. He's not my guru, but he is an indispensable source of information and fun. A lot of people perceive him as an over-grown hippie, but I see him as a hard-ass scholar, a subtle teacher and, of course, a poet."

In 1985, after the fame and the fortune that *Fup* provided, Dodge pulled up stakes in Cazadero and moved 240 miles or so up the California coast to Arcata. He insists that he "isn't permanent anywhere," but he has settled down on an old dairy farm – a short drive from Humboldt State University, where he teaches advanced fiction writing and the poetic imagination. His students have, of course, read his books, though he doesn't assign them. They have found them on their own.

It's late afternoon now and cars are starting to clog Mendocino Avenue. It's been a long interview, and Dodge is itching to beat rush hour traffic on 101. "After all these years I'm still exploring," he says. "I couldn't tell you the meaning of life. All I know is that I'm alive and that I'm going to make the best of it. Maybe there's a heaven. Maybe there's a hell – I don't know. But for sure I'm alive in this room. This moment here and now is what matters most."

Before he drives off, he reaches into the back seat of his car and autographs a copy of his latest volume of poetry, *Psalms to the Moon*. Only 100 copies have been printed, and the copy I receive is number ten. Obviously, the audience for the book of poems isn't going to be large, and that's okay with the author.

"If you are famous in your own community, what more could you want?" he asks. "It's all a question of scale. Andy Warhol used to say that after the revolution everyone would be famous for 15 minutes. I like to think that no one ought to be famous for more than three miles."

Freeman House

Totem Salmon:
Life Lessons from Another Species

Rivers run all around us. They even run through us in a manner of speaking. I understand that now, though I didn't when I first visited Free-man House at his home in Humboldt County. I had gone to talk about Abbie Hoffman – House had performed Abbie's hippie wedding ceremony, which *Time* magazine covered in 1967. While we were chatting about old times, House mentioned that he was involved in the "restoration of the Mattole." Unaware that the Mattole was – and still is – a river, and not conversant with bio-regionalism, I assumed that he was fixing up an architectural landmark – a 19th-century mansion perhaps – or even an old town on the "Lost Coast," that remote region in the northwest corner of California that has recently become synonymous – thanks to the Drug Enforcement Agency – with marijuana cultivation.

I only began to grasp what House meant by restoration when he took me to a swimming hole in the Mattole on a blazing July afternoon. (It was my baptism in the waters of bio-regionalism, I suppose, as well as a chance to cool off.) Sitting along the banks of the river, House explained that he and his neighbors in and around Petrolia were aiming to clean up the river and the surrounding landscape so that the once-abundant salmon might return to their old habitat after a long absence. The task of restoring a river, even a river as relatively minuscule as the Mattole, seemed Herculean. Where did it begin, I wondered? Where did it end? And what method could surmount the seemingly insurmountable obstacles contrived by human beings and nature itself?

Now, after nearly two decades of restoration and community-building – after co-founding the Mattole Restoration Council and the Mattole Watershed Salmon Support Group – House has written a very personal and very political book that provides the answers to all of my questions. *Totem Salmon* tells the story of the author's own life on, along, and literally in the Mattole River – and about the life and near-death of the river itself. A compact, elegantly written book, it is destined to become a contemporary classic in the fast-growing body of literature about habitat in California.

The Mattole River Basin, as House points out, is at the heart of the westernmost watershed in California. It is also the wettest place in the state. It rains eight to twelve feet a year, enough to make it seem as though all creatures, whether aquatic or terrestrial, are often underwater. Despite the fact that the basin does not have super highways, big cities or high-tech industries, it is a near-perfect microcosm to explore the environmental problems of the planet at large. Most of our economic, cultural and political problems exist there in miniature.

Part sociology, part biology and part anthropology, *Totem Salmon* presents a beautiful tapestry of a way of life close to the land that seems to be on the verge of extinction in northern California, and in nearly every other corner of the globe. House shows both the fragility and the resilience of the web of life. He makes the simple but often neglected point that everything on the face of the earth is connected, including Homo Sapiens and salmon, that amazing species that seems to have a built-in compass, calendar, map and clock that enables it to swim thousands of miles – from salt water to the freshwater rivers and streams where it was born.

Totem Salmon is an invitation to reexamine our basic ideas about ourselves and our place in the universe. It prompted me to review my own thoughts. As a boy I loved pseudo-scientific books that insisted that man is far wiser and far more adaptable than any other species. For most of my life I've endorsed that point of view – detractors call it "species chauvinism." If given a choice today I'd still rather be a human being than a fish, but after reading *Totem Salmon* I'm willing to admit that I may be able to learn from salmon, a species that is not only very intelligent, but also very determined to survive in the most adverse conditions, a prospect that seems likely to face human beings in the not too-distant future.

House describes his own heroic efforts to help salmon spawn and reproduce. With an endearing sense of humor, he describes himself as a social worker for the salmon, though no fish has ever asked for his help. Along with the humor, there's a sense of mystery, awe and spirituality. There are majestic passages, especially near the start of the book, in which the author describes himself standing in the Mattole River capturing female salmon bursting with eggs. *Totem Salmon* offers some of the most beautiful nature writing in contemporary California literature, and while it's hard to select one representative passage, perhaps this will serve: "If the salmon are running in the deep night in December or January, it is likely that the moon is new, that the river is rising, and that the water is clouded with silt. It is probably raining. The salmon will use these elements of obscurity to hide them from predators while they make a dash toward the spawning ground."

The salmon fish is the star of this show, but House also writes compassionately about a large cast of quirky human characters: the Native Americans who fished the Mattole for hundreds of years before Europeans arrived in northern California, and the mostly white settlers who have logged, hunted, ranched, fished and farmed, whether for legal or illegal crops, and who have often clashed with one another. *Totem Salmon* is insightful on the enmity and the amity that has existed over the past several decades between the ranchers and loggers – whose business practices often damaged the watershed – and the New Age folks who espouse ecological concerns. House himself belongs to the most recent wave of settlers, some of whom turned marijuana into their totem and the mainstay of their cottage industry. This book touches briefly on the outlaw marijuana economy of the region, but it is refreshing that marijuana – and law-enforcement efforts to eradicate it – take a back seat to salmon, and to issues of restoration, reforestation and the cultural evolution of the community as a whole.

Totem Salmon is about cooperation and collaboration. It sings the praises of "patience, humility, and mutuality." And so it offers a moral vision. It reminds me of William Hinton's *Fanshan* which focuses on one small village in rural China, and at the same time tells a story about the whole country. Northern California isn't, of course, China and the loggers, hippies and fishermen of the Lost Coast aren't peasants by any means. But *Totem Salmon* exhibits the same sort of respect for place – for its people, traditions and history. I know of no book that is more local than House's and no book that is more global in its implications. It's too bad that salmon aren't book literate and can't read about themselves in these pages. As for the rest of us, there's just no good excuse for not making space for House's book on reading tables.

Freeman House: The Fisher King

Fish and fishing have long played a hefty part in Freeman House's adventurous life. His father made it a point to teach him how to fish as a young boy, and as an adult he has earned a living as a commercial fisherman all along the Pacific Coast – from Shelter Cover to Puget Sound and then in Alaska, where he was struck by the superabundance of the natural world. "It was a revelation," House says during a Saturday morning phone conversation from his solar-powered home near the Mattole River. "I fell in love with salmon," he adds. "Salmon ignited my imagination; they have a profound influence on anyone who gets near them." No wonder that House has adopted salmon as his totem.

Born in Anaheim before there was a Disneyland, and when there were still acres of orange groves, he remembers that his parents bought fresh eggs and milk from neighboring farmers. Later, his family moved to the town of Walnut Creek, when the population was piddling and when there were still wild salmon in the creek that ran through the grounds of the high school. "I spent a lot of time along the creek," House says. "It was an important place to escape to. But I graduated from school without knowing how to appreciate the landscape right outside the classroom. Not a single science teacher thought it was important to teach us about the salmon in the creek."

After he graduated from high school, House wandered about the country feeling alienated from the landscape and with "a profound sense of emptiness." Decades later, he discovered that for his own personal happiness he needed to be in close relationship to the land. After that it wasn't a big step to realize that human beings as a species need a connection to place in order to feel fully human.

In the 1960s, House went to UC Berkeley and majored in English and theater. When the counterculture sprang up, seemingly overnight, he joined the Diggers, one of the most creative theatrical/political groups in San Francisco, and lived without frills in the midst of material abundance. Like many radicals who demonstrated against the Vietnam War, and against the establishment as a whole, House adopted the confrontational, in-your-face style that succeeded in polarizing the country, if in nothing else. It was an attitude that stuck with him for years, and it took years to break away from it, and adopt a less combative way of being in the world.

"I was pulled kicking and screaming into consensus politics, which I saw at first simply as a New Age gimmick," he says. "What impelled me to alter my behavior was the fact that I felt physically and emotionally uncomfortable going to the local store in Petrolia. I spent a year creating a safe place to talk about community with my own neighbors." And he adds, "I found that the hardest people to talk to, and also the people it was most important to talk to, were the people who lived next door."

Few individuals have done as much to create community – that living web that brings together people and place – as House has done in Humboldt County. "It's essential that people living in common figure out, on their own, the terms of their daily activity and their life style," he says. "Weaving the web of community is as important as legislative reform and wilderness preservation."

Roy Parvin

In the Snow Forest

Sometimes the cover of a book lures me inside – and it's not necessarily a sexy cover. With Roy Parvin's *In the Snow Forest*, it was the picture of the snow-filled woods. Outside, on my redwood deck, it was 102, and too hot to do much of anything except read and sip on a cold drink.

Once I was inside the book the blazing sun seemed to have disappeared and that, I suppose, is a tribute to the power of Parvin's prose and to the world it creates. Read these beautifully crafted tales – call them long short stories or very short novels – and you're transported to a place that's chilling and invigorating and emotionally comforting as well. They're strange and mysterious and haunting, all at once.

The three novellas that are collected here stake out their own separate territories and yet they have much in common. All of them are about men and women in transit, and in one way or another, on the road and in flight from something or somebody – often themselves. Parvin's people – loggers, thieves, killers, artists and writers – are lonely, isolated, driven, most of them in pursuit of salvation, redemption, a vital connection to other human beings.

"In the Snow Forest," the title story, appears second in the volume and serves as a kind of ballast or anchor for the book as a whole. Set in the chilly woods of northern California, it explores loss and recovery, disappearance and reappearance. The main characters here are Darby and Harper. He's a logger and "the last of his line." She's a nurse who tells "crazy stories" and lives an even crazier life. Their paths – like the paths of Parvin's other quirky characters – intersect and become entangled before they go their separate ways.

At times, *In the Snow Forest* put me in mind of Jack London. Like London, Parvin writes about men in the wilderness, and like London, there's a sense of raw power, as in this passage: "That fall the Trinities were empty of men. Darby the only one left. The only one who didn't sign on with the logging teams when a private timber concern came through back in August, an outfit operating north out of Cecilville, high and far in the granite hills, the rare opportunity to fell the big sticks till the first snows." There are echoes of London, but Parvin writes more tenderly. His characters evolve emotionally and they even mature. There are no reversions to savagery here.

Parvin's first story, which is entitled "Betty Hutton," and the third story, which is entitled "Menno's Granddaughter," are in a way mirror images of one another. Both are about characters who are running from the past, moving on instinct. In "Betty Hutton," an ex-convict named Gibbs steals a car in New Jersey and frantically heads west. In "Menno's Granddaughter," an attractive young woman named Lindsay travels east by train from California to New York. Gibbs and Lindsay are on opposite ends of the continent, but they're both driven, both trying to unravel their knotted lives. Both of them interrupt their journeys just long enough to meet strangers, make friends and make peace with themselves.

The climactic scenes in "Betty Hutton" and in "Menno's Granddaughter" take place during blizzards. Gibbs becomes a "prisoner of snow" and Lindsay finds herself "locked in the ice chest of winter." Both of them break free from their confining selves. Gibbs continues his journey west and Lindsay heads east. And the book provides a sense of pleasing symmetry.

"Menno's Granddaughter" has inspiring moments, and yet it didn't touch me as deeply as either of the first two stories. Maybe that's because Parvin seems better at describing men and women on the margins than he is at describing people caught in the middle of things. When he writes about Gibbs's frantic world, his prose seems positively inspired: "It was lovely – he had no other words to match up with the landscape – only lovely and cold. The lake looked even colder yet and it stretched out before him glassy as a marble, the smudge of twilight already descending, the surrounding mountains holding a few clouds within their spires like a cage."

Whether they're about women in love or men who barely know how to talk about love, these stories are for all sorts of readers and for all seasons. Roy Parvin's novellas are as good as they get in American fiction today.

Roy Parvin: When Reading is an Act of Creation

Long before he began to write fiction, Roy Parvin was devouring huge tracts of literature. By the time he was a 10-year-old boy growing up in suburban New Jersey, he was spending hours curled up with *The New Yorker*, his favorite magazine. "These days college students want to become writers, but they don't want to read," Parvin said during a phone conversation from his home in remote Humboldt County. "If you want to write, you've got to read. It's essential. For a writer, reading is a creative act. You study how a story works, how it's put together, like a scientist doing a lab experiment."

From the time he was a child, Parvin wanted to be a writer, but no one encouraged him, not in high school and not at Swathmore, the small liberal arts college in Pennsylvania where he studied history as an undergraduate. He's never enrolled in a creative writing program. It wasn't until 1993 – when he was already 36 years old – that he finally knew that he had to write, come what may.

"When I decided to become a writer I was ready," he says. "I was both open and innocent. Moreover, I had experience and perceptions and energy. A lot of people I meet have romantic ideas about writing. They think they'll put on a beret and become famous overnight. I found that to be a real writer you've got to show up at your desk and do the work everyday, like a job."

For years, Parvin wrote short stories and for years he thought that his destiny was to write short stories. *The Loneliest Road in America*, his first collection of short stories, won enough literary acclaim and provided him with enough incentive for him to go on writing in the same genre. But he found himself turning out longer and longer stories, and before he knew it, he was enjoying the newfound freedom afforded by the novella.

"My short stories tend to be plot-driven," Parvin says. "The dramatic tension is usually born of a situation. The novellas are different; they're character-driven. Then, too, in a short story, I always hear a clock ticking. In the novella I can suspend that feeling and dive into a character much more deeply."

Many of the characters in Parvin's novellas are on the edge. You have the feeling that they might go off on a rampage, without warning, like so many of the violent characters in contemporary road fiction and film. "I deliberately didn't want to write that kind of story," he says. "It has been done over and over again, and by now those stories of men going berserk are clichéd. Still, I do enjoy putting my characters in extreme situations that will test their mettle."

Living in Humboldt County seems to have helped Parvin to find his identity as a writer. "Life is pleasanter here than in San Francisco, where I used to live," he says. "It's slower, and I like that better. The people in Humboldt are a lot closer than the people in San Francisco to the kinds of characters that I write about. And of course the solitary life of the writer suits me just fine."

Is there anything else he wants to say? There's a pause on the phone before he adds, *"In the Snow Forest* is a book you can read by a fire. I picture that. I also wrote these stories in hopes that people would read them more than once. There are echoes and reverberations and depths that might not be apparent right away."

Gerald Haslam

Coming of Age in California

If the home team often has the advantage on the baseball diamond, so too the home writer often has the advantage over the visiting writer in the field of literature. But it often takes more than feeling at home to succeed as a writer. The local writer – the writer with roots – may need an edge: the sense of being an underdog and going against the odds.

For most of his literary life, Gerald Haslam has had the confidence that comes from being a home writer. Plus he's had the spunk of the underdog. It's a winning combination, and it's apparent in *Coming of Age in California*, a collection of personal essays that was originally published a decade ago and that was selected recently by northern California readers as one of the 20th century's best non-fiction books from the West. *Coming of Age* has just been reissued with six new essays and a new preface by the author. From 90 pages the book has grown to 142, and it has gotten richer in the process.

Almost everywhere in this volume, and most obviously in the essay entitled, "A Lesson from Home," Haslam writes about places that are deeply embedded in his soul: Oildale, his home town; the Great Central Valley, his home territory; and California, his home state. The people who show up in the essays entitled "Pop," "An Affair of Love," and "Portrait of a Pal" are family members and old friends. There doesn't seem to be a subject – whether it's his own prostate cancer or an ex-girlfriend – that he's uncomfortable writing about, and though Haslam writes from the heart, he also writes with a sense of humor, as in "Fleas on Board," a 1999 essay that's about the dogs in his life.

If he's at home in the subjects he writes about, he can also be feisty. So, in the title essay, "Coming of Age in California," he explains that he has never been willing "to concede power to anyone." Why? Perhaps because, as he himself explains in the preface to the second edition, he was "the only child of a working-class family during the Great Depression." Moreover, he came of age in a locale that didn't seem to have much culture, at least not the kind of culture that counts in what are called cosmopolitan centers. The odds were against Haslam to emerge as a writer. They were also against his neighbors and schoolmates. And so these personal essays are compelling because Haslam speaks for folks like himself who grew up in small towns and in farming communities and who often felt they were unseen and invisible.

The author's sense of native defiance and local pride is perhaps best expressed in "Writing About Home," an illuminating essay on the challenges that face regional writers in the big national literary scene. "A region is also subversive, for with it may come rootedness, tradition and values," Haslam writes. "It resists and mitigates change while the center subsumes threatening variations." "Writing About Home" offers practical advice to writers, whether they're veterans or beginners. "How do you write about home?" Haslam asks. "You can't pander to the prejudice of editors in Beverly Hills or New York, nor can you indulge local illusions or pretensions." I don't know anyone who has said it more succinctly.

Reading *Coming of Age in California* reminded me of my own experience teaching literature in Europe a few years ago. Most of the students had slick images of Californians – buffed bodies, flabby minds – that were derived from Hollywood movies and TV soap operas. "You can't have culture in the sun!" was the way one man put it. Haslam's essays ought to be exported to those Europeans whose imaginations have been tainted by our mass produced culture. Yes, many of us have less-than-perfect bodies. Yes, many of us work in the fields, and yes, we do read and write books. And perhaps *Coming of Age in California* ought to be distributed locally, as well as exported. Santa Rosa Junior College might make this collection of essays required reading. After all, it's about time Haslam was accorded the recognition he deserves in his own backyard.

Haslam at Home: "I Still Have Aspirations"

His bags are packed and he's ready to travel by train and bus to Yosemite for a conference of bigwigs. But for an hour or so on this breezy afternoon in June, Gerald Haslam relaxes on the deck of his home in Penngrove, where he lives with his wife Jan and their dog Sammy who is too shy to come out from the shade of the oak and olive trees. In the distance you can hear the racket from a neighbor's chainsaw and the rumble of Friday traffic on Adobe Road. It's hardly a quiet setting for the author of 20 books, almost all of them written in Sonoma County.

Haslam has been retired for years from the English Department at Sonoma State University, but his life has not slowed down, not with so many stories inside him still waiting to be told. He's written *Straight White Male,* a novel about three generations in a northern California family and wouldn't you know it! Haslam is already in the creative throes of writing another novel.

"It's called *Walking the Plank,* and it's about a newspaper reporter named Marty Martinez whose life comes apart," Haslam explains. "His wife disappears without a trace, and he tries to find her with the help of his daughter. At the same time, he's surprised to discover that he's in love with a woman who is a breast cancer survivor. I haven't figured out who the wife is, or what she does and I don't know yet how the story is going to end."

These days the characters in Haslam's novels, short stories and essays tend to be men and women who came of age decades ago, and now are quickly aging. Not surprisingly, Haslam himself is getting older and becoming increasingly aware of what he calls "the inevitable, undeniable break-down of the body." Still, he doesn't look or act like an old man, not when he walks with his dog, rides his bicycle from Penngrove to Cotati, or dashes off to Yosemite. "What surprises me about getting older is how young I feel," he says. "Being alive fascinates me. I still have aspirations, I am still curious, still sexual, still ambitious, still working out."

He's still fascinated by his own youth in Oildale, but he's also curious about the generation that's just now beginning to flex its muscles in business, politics and the media. "The generations that have come of age after Vietnam and the 1960s are unlike my own generation in many ways," he says. "These days the breakdown in authority is a starting point. Individuals in the post-1960s generations have abundance of opportunity, and a feeling that they can ascend economically. Moreover, they seem to be born with a concern for social issues, especially racism and the environment."

Those same concerns loom large in Haslam's essays. Moreover, they are at the heart of two projects that are on backburners. One is a biography of S.I. Hawakawa, the controversial Japanese-American author, educator and politician who served as the president of San Francisco State and later in the U.S. Senate. Haslam's other project is a book abut the Carizzo Plain, a spectacular ecological niche in the Great Central Valley that straddles Kern and San Luis Obispo counties. When these books might move to front burners, Haslam isn't sure.

"Writing is a process of discovery for me," he says. "I don't chart everything I do. I don't use index cards, and I never start out with an outline of the story or the plot. You know, I never did take one of those courses in creative writing at college. And just maybe I didn't have to."

Diane di Prima

Loba

When was the last time you heard poetry on prime time TV? I can't remember poetry ever displacing Monday Night Football or the evening news. But now and again – miracle of miracles – poetry emerges from bohemian lofts and bourgeois haunts to descend on Main Street. And when that happens it's earthshaking. You feel transported to ancient times when poets sang of gods and goddesses, when there was dance and magic, and the mingling of wild men and wild women.

Probably no one writing poetry in northern California today recreates the wildness of ancient times with more raw power than Diane di Prima. And probably no woman poet today writes more lyrically or imaginatively about feminine and feminist landscapes. Di Prima, who was born in Brooklyn, New York in 1934, and who has lived in northern California for the last 30 years, is in the midst of a publishing revival that is bringing her work to the attention of a much wider audience than she has previously enjoyed. At long last, she's winning recognition from readers and from sister-poets like Adrienne Rich and Marge Piercy.

Today there's more di Prima to choose from than ever before. If you're looking for an introduction to her work, there's *Pieces of a Song*. If you want to read her early experimental prose (as well as early love poetry) there's *Dinners and Nightmares*. *Memoirs of a Beatnik*, her erotic account of her own coming-of-age in the era of the bomb and the Beats, recreates a sense of what it was like to be a young woman and an aspiring poet in the 1950s. Then, too there's an expanded version of *Loba*, di Prima's long epic poem that explores the archetype of the wolf goddess and maps the landscape of female experience and consciousness.

Di Prima's autobiography, *Recollections of My Life as a Woman*, takes readers from her early years in a large Italian-American family to the exuberant 1960s when she founded the avant garde Poets Press and the New York Poets Theater, and was intimately involved with LeRoi Jones, Jack Kerouac and Allen Ginsberg.

I talked with di Prima about her unconventional life and her experimental work – her poetry, her sense of place, and about the Petaluma Poetry Walk, which was founded by local poet and impresario Geri Digiorno, and already a cultural institution with local citizens and Bay Area literati.

When we spoke on a warm Friday afternoon, di Prima was at her home in San Francisco's outer Mission district. She had just returned from teaching a poetry workshop in Petaluma, and she was on her way to a meditation retreat at the Sonoma Mountain Zen Center.

"When I was in high school in the 1940s, I was taught that there was only one right way to write poetry," she said. "That was the T.S. Eliot way. Now young poets have a whole world of choices. There are so many different things happening. There's street poetry and poetry slams, oral and improvised poetry, the language poets, and the new formalism. There's everything happening under the sun and that's exciting."

Di Prima began to write poetry at age 7, when most girls her generation were still playing with dolls. By the time she was a teenager, she knew that poetry would play a major part in her life. "I committed to poetry when I was 14," she says. "I loved the romantic poets, though they were scorned by most of my teachers." In rebellion against the academic idea of what poetry was supposed to be, she began to find her own voice. "Sometimes having something to rebel against is useful," she says.

After two years as an undergraduate at Swarthmore, she dropped out of college and moved to Greenwich Village, the poetry capital of America. Di Prima has kept moving ever since, spiritually as well as geographically, rebelling against conventional ways of seeing and doing, venturing into uncharted spaces, combining the reverential and the irreverent.

Landscapes often figure in her poetry, and landscapes often inspire her work. In *Revolutionary Letters*, a collection of overtly political poems which was first published in 1971, the landscape is distinctly urban. The language sounds as though it has sprung directly from the gritty, raucous life of the city, and indeed as di Prima explains, the poems that make up *Revolutionary Letters* were originally written to be performed on the streets of New York.

Loba is something else again. The first part of the poem was written when di Prima lived in Marshall in a house on stilts that sat above Tomales Bay. In many ways it was an isolated existence at the edge of the continent, a long, long way from the madness of Manhattan. In west Marin, she discovered a kind of tranquillity, especially when she walked "the russet and purple and young green hills." The contours of the land influenced her writing as much as the rhythms of the tide at Marshall. "I'd sleep out on the land," she says. "That land is in the poems. It's a grail-like landscape in which any kind of quest is possible."

Don't read *Loba* expecting photographic images of northern California. The landscapes are global and galactic, rather than local and familiar. Sometimes you feel you're on a strange and distant planet, or in a dark cave, or in Medieval times. *Loba* transports you into a world of magic and mythology, archetypal mothers and legendary daughters – Aphrodite, Demeter, Beatrice and Guinevere. The poetry has a hypnotic power, a seductive appeal, an awesome sense of eternal sky, infinite stars, unchanging earth.

"The energy of landscape and of sky and sea, and how it works in us, is what *Loba* is about," di Prima says. "All the poems in the book are connected. They explore a woman's inner journey."

Di Prima often hears her poems in her own head before she writes them down. She rarely revises and she doesn't worry about making explicit connections or explaining transitions.

"I didn't know that *Loba* would be a long poem when I started out," she says. "But I love long poems. And I love to juxtapose different kinds of experience."

Alicia Bay Laurel

Living on the Earth

Living on the Earth was originally published in 1970 – the year of the first Earth Day, and the invasion of Cambodia, and the year the National Guard killed four students at Kent State. Nineteen seventy was a good year to lie low, a year that Alicia Bay Laurel lived on a commune in western Sonoma County.

I think of *Living on the Earth* as "that '70s book." Indeed, it captures the countercultural lifestyle of the 1970s – the lifestyle that many people associate with the 1960s. *Living on the Earth* is about going back to the land and living naturally and playfully. When it finally went out of print in 1980, it had sold more than 350,000 copies.

Folks on communes read it, as well as curious middle class moms and dads in suburbia who wanted to know what their wayward sons and daughters were doing in the boonies, besides smoking marijuana and having sex. Laurel's book was just what city and suburban kids needed in the 1970s when they left home or dropped out of college and moved to the countryside. It told them how to be hippies – how to cook inexpensive, healthy food and how to keep house, even in a yurt, and how to make simple clothes. It showed how to be independent, how to live without mom and dad, and most of all, how to live without the mall. Written in a graceful hand – this book looks like a personal journal – and easy to read, it provides practical information about homesteading and farming. It also offers beautiful drawings by the author herself of naked girls and boys in an Edenic landscape – all of which make the rigors of rural living look like pure unadulterated fun.

Now, at the start of the millennium, with third-generation hippies quickly coming of age, Laurel's book is back in print in a new, revised 30th anniversary edition that's more environmentally sensitive than the original. This time the author doesn't suggest bathing in streams. The streams aren't as clean as they once were. And she doesn't suggest cutting down trees in the forest to make the human habitat either. The forests are a lot thinner now than they were in the 1970s, and the trees are fewer and farther between. There are other changes in the text, but overall the joyous down-to-earth feeling of the original has been preserved. The idealistic values of the counterculture come through as loudly and as clearly as ever before. Eden is still possible. Utopia is right around the next hillside.

It's hard to believe that *Living on the Earth* will sell as well in the coming decade as it did in the 1970s. Today it seems in part like a cultural artifact from a long-ago decade. It's a work of nostalgia now, not a practical workbook. Still, it has an undeniable charm and innocence, and it's likely to make some readers long to escape from news of today's downwardly spiraling stock market and escape into a simpler, quieter, seemingly less competitive era. For those hardy utopians who are still around and looking for blueprints, *Living on the Earth* is likely to provide inspiration, once again, to live in harmony with the planet and all its sentient beings.

Alicia Bay Laurel: Bohemian

Alicia Bay Laurel is back in Sebastopol – this afternoon at Lucy's Restaurant on Main Street. Lucy's wasn't here when Laurel lived in Sonoma County in the 1970s, and Sebastopol never had this much traffic or this much noise either. A lot has changed. Alicia Bay Laurel has changed, and yet she's remained the same. "I'm not living on the land anymore," she says. "But I'm the same old girl. I'm still eating tofu and sprouts. I still love the life style that I describe in the book – I had a great time then – and that's why I wanted the old book to be in print again."

Alicia Bay Laurel was born Alice Carla Kaufman in Los Angeles. She grew up in a Jewish family with a leftist slant, though her parents were a bit secretive about their radical politics in the 1950s, when Senator Joseph McCarthy investigated everybody and everything, including the U.S. Army. As a young woman, Alice Kaufman went to civil rights protests and played folk music and wrote folk songs, too. She loved Bob Dylan and Mose Allison. If one word might describe her then, that word would be "beatnik." In 1966, she left L.A. to attend San Francisco State and to throw herself into the beatnik scene in North Beach. That's where she gave herself the name Alicia Bay Laurel, because it sounded feminine and watery and natural.

Alicia lived in the Haight-Ashbury just as the hippies were busy being born, and she observed the phenomenon as it rose and fell. Later, she moved to Bill Wheeler's ranch – the hippie Mecca – outside Occidental, and that's where she wrote large parts of *Living on the Earth*, which she describes as "a rural, feminine version of Abbie Hoffman's urban macho text, *Steal This Book*."

"I was fearless in those days," she says. "I was passionately artistic and in love with being outdoors in nature. I'd hitchhike anywhere, take drugs without thinking, and do things with people I didn't know."

At 50, Alicia Bay Laurel still seems fearless. She's traveling across the country all by herself to promote her book and to take a reading on the state of American culture. When she's finished her cross-continental travels, she's planning to write a book with the working title, *Living on the Road: Bohemians and the Millennium.* The idea is to write about alternative life styles at the start of the 21st century.

Alicia Bay Laurel doesn't call herself a hippie. She never really did. She was almost always a bohemian and she still considers herself a bohemian. And what does bohemian mean to her? "It means that the relationship between the physical world and the spiritual world is endlessly fascinating," she says. "It means putting compassion for people ahead of profits, and that freedom and self-expression are more important than conforming to the rules."

Part II:
California Dreams,
California Nightmares

Greg Sarris

Watermelon Nights

The way I figure it, there are three sorts of Sonoma County writers. First, those who live here and write about this part of the world, like Robin Beeman. Second, those who live here and write about other places, such as Lynn Freed. And third, those writers like Greg Sarris who live elsewhere but write about this place.

In case you need reminding, Sarris is the author of *Grand Avenue*, a collection of innovative short stories that was turned into an HBO movie by Robert Redford and filmed here in 1996. The "bastard" son – as he has called himself – of a Jewish mother and a Filipino/Indian father, Sarris was adopted soon after his birth in 1952, and was raised by a white middle class family in the Montecito Heights area of Santa Rosa. As a boy, he gravitated to Santa Rosa's South Park ("a convenient place for the town to stash its skeletons," he says), and felt at home among the Indian, Portuguese and Mexican families.

These days Sarris lives in Los Angeles, and armed with a Ph.D., teaches English at UCLA. He's a long way from his roots in Sonoma County, and yet Sonoma County is at the heart of all his fiction. His novel, *Watermelon Nights*, which traces three generations in a family of Indians, is a bittersweet love song to Sonoma County and to the world at large.

Sarris is especially well-suited to write about us. After all he's part of the extended Sonoma County family, an insider who has the kind of familiarity that an artist needs in order to recreate flesh-and-blood characters. At the same time he's an outsider – an exile in L.A. – and that distance and accompanying detachment makes it possible for him to describe the big social picture that we expect from a major work of fiction.

Sarris knows Sonoma County history better than anyone I know, save for Gaye LeBaron, who doesn't appear as a character in *Watermelon Nights*, but who is a topic of conversation in these pages. "Gaye LeBaron," one Indian woman says to another, "she tells about the goings-on." Much of the charm of Sarris's novel comes from the mention of local people, like Gaye LeBaron, local communities like Graton and Sebastopol, and even specific streets from Fourth Street to Grand and MacDonald Avenues. Reading *Watermelon Nights*, I felt that I was Greg Sarris's invisible sidekick and that I was right there listening to his characters as they tell their own life stories in their own unique voices.

Over the last few years Sarris has matured as a writer. *Grand Avenue*, his first published work of fiction, is very good indeed. *Watermelon Nights* is even better. Promoted as a "novel in stories," *Grand Avenue* comes across as a collection of related tales, rather than as a unified novel. *Watermelon Nights* is the real thing. It's far more ambitious – it's at least twice as long and far more intricate – as intricate and as durable, one might say, as a Pomo Indian basket. It's more autobiographical than *Grand Avenue*, and at the same time it's on a larger, grander scale. If *Grand Avenue* sometimes reads like a series of episodes on prime-time TV, then *Watermelon Nights* reads like an epic.

History is at the heart of the novel – Indian history, California history, American history, from the Depression through World War II to our own era. I imagine that critics will label this a California novel, or an Indian novel, as though it belongs in a neat regional or ethnic category. I prefer to think of it as an American novel. Sarris has burrowed so deeply into our region that he's hit the bedrock of our national experience. He's made Sonoma County into a metaphor for the nation at large.

Watermelon Nights has three main characters – Johnny Gonzales, who is part Indian, part white; his grandmother Elba, who maintains the old Indian ways despite a cultural onslaught; and Johnny's mother, Iris, who tries to blend into the white world, and loses much of her Indian identity.

When the novel opens, Johnny is 20 and on the verge of leaving his Santa Rosa home and going off to the big city life in San Francisco. Though he isn't a Xerox copy of young Greg Sarris, Johnny Gonzales seems a lot like the author, and in writing about him Sarris explores some of the thorny sides of his own self – his sexuality as well as his ethnicity.

The second section of *Watermelon Nights* – the longest in the book – belongs to Elba who relates her story, and the story of her tribe as it is driven from its ancestral lands, and as individual members are scattered every which way. It isn't a pretty picture: there's theft, rape, suicide and the violation of a culture. Moreover, the Indian characters aren't simply the hapless victims of whites. Indeed, they're often accomplices in their own undoing. Elba is beaten down again and again, and yet she salvages her dignity. After a series of miscarriages, she finally gives birth to a daughter, gets a steady job and buys a house of her own.

Despite the bitterness of injustice, there is always, in Sarris's world, the sweetness of watermelon nights, those moments when everyone in the community comes into the street for a spontaneous fiesta. Then too, there's the kind of Indian humor that makes the film *Smoke Signals* – which is based on Sherman Alexis's novel, *The Lone Ranger and Tonto Fistfight in Heaven* – so refreshing. "White people. Can't live with them, can't live without them," one of Sarris's characters quips.

The third and last part of the novel – Iris's section – is the part I like the best, probably because it conjures up the 1950s, an era I lived through and still remember. Iris graduates from Santa Rosa High School, gets married and moves to Montecito Heights, a million miles culturally from the South Park world of her own mother. Sarris writes especially well about Iris's teenage years; he knows what it feels like to have a crush, to go on a date, to have the sexual energy of youth.

He also has a knack for reversing the familiar point of view. Repeatedly, he takes you into the broken-down shed, the cramped maid's quarters and lets you peer through the window at the people in the big house. The novel is an invitation to see the world through the eyes of the outcast, the dispossessed and the disinherited. A sense of compassion infuses the work as a whole, and that means compassion no matter what the skin color of the characters. Even Mr. and Mrs. Polk, their son Patrick and their daughter Mary Beth – Sarris's version of the WASP family – are treated with respect.

Watermelon Nights comes full circle; it ends where it began with Johnny Gonzales on the brink of a new life, and with the Indians of South Park on the verge of coming together again. It's an aesthetically satisfying conclusion that sends you back to the beginning, and then perhaps to read the novel all over again. It's that good – a novel by one of our own for all of America.

Greg Sarris: "The Voices of the Characters Took Over"

Greg Sarris is in area code 213. I'm in area code 707. We're hundreds of miles apart, but I can hear the nervousness in his voice as soon as he picks up the phone and says, "Greg Sarris." Before long he explains, "I woke up last night and began to worry about this interview. I know I should be more worried about talking with *The New York Times* than about doing this interview, but this interview is important. People in my home town are going to read this; they're the people who really matter."

Santa Rosa is still Greg Sarris's home town, and he still loves it dearly. "My childhood was good training for becoming a writer," he says. "I learned to read situations and people." And yet, after all these years, Sarris still feels angry about "stuff," as he puts it, about the way that he was mistreated as a kid, and about the way that Santa Rosa mistreated the Indians of South Park. But time has a way of mellowing, if not healing, almost everything.

"There were people who didn't want to have anything to do with me when I was growing up because I was a greaser, a street kid, a bad boy," he says. "Now their sons and daughters want to have dinner with me and that's okay."

Sarris didn't read much as a kid, but by the 11th grade he began to put his life together and that meant reading fiction, as well as studying for exams. "Reading William Faulkner was incredibly important to me," he says. "I read his short stories first, and later I moved on to his novels – *The Sound and the Fury*, *Light in August*, and my favorite, *Absalom, Absalom!* To me, Faulkner is about people talking, which is something I knew from listening to the story tellers – and to all the gossip – I heard in South Park." Listening to stories in South Park proved to be the starting point for *Watermelon Nights*. "During the filming of *Grand Avenue,* I heard a story about a watermelon truck that was parked over on Grand Avenue," he says. "Everyone in the community took melons off that truck and ate them for days. Later, sitting at home, I began to think about that event. It took on mythological proportions, and I decided to build my novel around it."

Like Faulkner's work, Sarris's work reverberates with myth and legend. Unlike Faulkner, however, who created a mythological county in Mississippi that he called Yoknapatawpha, Sarris has been content to work with Sonoma County and use real place names.

"In writing *Watermelon Nights*, I wanted to take an actual place and create a fictional history for it," he says. "Fiction is always more illuminating to me than just the facts. Whenever I listen to Gaye LeBaron talk about local history, I find myself wanting to know what people in the past were thinking and feeling, and how the facts fit into a larger story."

From the time he was a boy in Santa Rosa, Sarris has had a keen sense of where he belongs culturally. Recently he's given a lot of thought to his place in the latest Native American literary renaissance. "Sherman Alexie is very hot right now," Sarris says. "He sees a 1960s kind of polarization between 'reds' and 'whites,' and his characters tend to be cartoonish. I'm more serious; my characters are more complicated. Then there's Louise Erdrich. I think I'm closer to her, though I'm not as lyrical as she is, and I'm not as dependent on metaphor and symbol."

Writing *Watermelon Nights* proved to be a learning experience for Sarris. "I tend to be a control freak," he says. "But with this new book I lost control at times. The voices of the characters took over. It was like being on the back of a wild horse. I held on and went with it."

Though Sarris left Sonoma County a long time ago, he still returns again and again, and he looks forward to his homecomings. "I'm the chairman of the Coast Miwok tribe, so I can't ever get too far away," he says. "The next time I'm up there, I want to go back to South Park and eat fry-bread with friends."

Isabel Allende

Portrait in Sepia

Isabel Allende has lived in exile from her native Chile ever since 1975, when a military coup toppled the government of President Salvador Allende, her own uncle – and forced her as well as thousands of others to flee the country. She's been an "outsider in California" – as she calls herself – since she settled in Marin in 1987.

Not surprisingly, she began to write novels about outsiders, exiles and immigrants soon after her arrival here. Her fictional characters are often Chilean, but they're also from almost everywhere else on the face of the earth: China, Scotland, England, Australia and Eastern Europe.

There are no overt messages in Allende's fiction and no blatant morals in her stories. But if you read between the lines, what she seems to be saying is that California is a country of the world and that it's a country that has been and still is shaped by its outsiders, exiles and immigrants. Moreover, Allende's California can be a living hell as well as the Promised Land.

For Aurora del Valle, the 19th-century heroine of *Portrait in Sepia*, California is a place of social extremes – from lowly Chinatown to the elite world atop Nob Hill. A photographer and a creative writer, she experiences, and then describes, those extremes in both word and image. *Portrait in Sepia* is the traumatic tale of her own life in California, and the epic tale of her own multicultural family, which appeared for the first time in *House of the Spirits* (1982), a brilliant novel that explores a century of Chilean history and politics. The del Valle family also appears in *Daughter of Fortune*, which takes place during the California Gold Rush, when, as one character observes, California became a "paradise of greed."

Portrait in Sepia extends the saga of the sprawling del Valle clan. The novel begins in 1862, nearly two decades before Aurora's own birth in San Francisco. It ends in 1910, when she's 30 years old and living in Santiago, Chile, the land of her ancestors. You might call *Portrait* a historical novel – since much of it is set in Chile in the 19th century. Oddly enough, however, there's very little American or California history, though the era from 1862 to 1910 is ripe for historical fiction.

Aurora herself seems more like a woman of the present day transported back to the Victorian past with all the appropriate costumes. Haunted by the ghosts of childhood events and emotionally scarred by a marriage to an unfaithful husband, she's a genuinely sympathetic character and modern readers are likely to feel inspired by the story of her own emancipation.

Unfortunately, it takes nearly 100 pages for Aurora to make her grand entrance in the pages of the novel. Before she appears on stage, Allende introduces a vast cast of characters – enough for at least two or three novels. Here are just some of them: Aurora's own father Matias del Valle, an opium addict and a Latin playboy who runs off with a Scottish actress named Amanda Lowell; Aurora's mother Lynn, who dies in childbirth; Aurora's grandmother Paulina, the matriarch of the California branch of the del Valle family, who adopts the orphaned Aurora and also marries her own butler, an escaped convict from Australia. There are more: Aurora's Chinese grandfather Tao Chi'en, a doctor who is brutally beaten to death by thugs in San Francisco; Aurora's husband Diego who is in love with his sister-in-law Susana; and Aurora's own charismatic lover, Dr. Ivan Radovic, an immigrant from Eastern Europe who looks like Genghis Khan. If you're an English teacher and you want a novel with diverse characters, this book may be for you. If you're the common reader, you might want a chart to keep track of the immense cast of characters.

Portrait in Sepia isn't one of Allende's best novels. Part of the problem may be that there isn't enough historical detail here. Though the novel takes place from 1862-1910, there's no mention of the American Civil War, Reconstruction, or even the earthshaking California earthquake of 1906. There is a lot of Chilean history, but that history is peripheral to the main plot and dramatic action.

It may also be that Allende is simply writing too quickly. In the past decade she's produced five big books: *The Infinite Plan*, a novel set in contemporary Los Angeles; *Paula*, a memoir about the life and the death of her own daughter; *Aphrodite*, a coquettish volume about food and sex; and her two California-inspired novels, *Daughter of Fortune* and now *Portrait in Sepia*.

In the early 1970s, Pablo Neruda, the Chilean poet, scolded Isabel Allende –who was then working as a journalist – for inventing the news and for putting herself at the center of every story she wrote. "Why don't you write novels instead," he said. "In literature those defects are virtues." By the end of the 1970s, when she was living in exile in Venezuela, Allende began to follow Neruda's advice and to write fiction – though she did not abandon journalism.

Her finest work – *The House of the Spirits* – is based in part on diligent research, interviews and news gathering. Allende seems to work best when her imagination absorbs fact and turns it into fiction – and when it recasts history as myth. Her 1999 novel, *Daughter of Fortune,* is fascinating because it offers a unique perspective on the role of outsiders and exiles – especially the Chileans and the Chinese – in the California Gold Rush. *Portrait in Sepia* could use more history, and a deeper and more abiding sense of California as a real and as a magical land.

Interview with Isabel Allende: A Wandering Pilgrim

Jonah: How did *Portrait in Sepia* originate?
Isabel: My original idea was to write a novel about the wars that took place in Chile in the 19th century, a time when the Chilean national character was formed. There was brutal torture, people disappeared and many flew into exile. It was a foreshadowing of the coup of 1973. When General Pinochet took over people asked, "How could this happen here?" It already had.

At the same time I was thinking how I could connect *Portrait in Sepia* to my previous novel *Daughter of Fortune*. Oprah Winfrey and others didn't like the open ending of *Daughter of Fortune*. They wanted a sequel. I don't like sequels because many readers will not have read the first book and so they're lost in the second book. *Portrait in Sepia* provided a way for me to continue the story I'd created in *Daughter of Fortune*.
Jonah: Are you going to write more about the del Valle family?
Isabel: No! I hate them!
Jonah: After living in California for more than a decade, do you feel at home here?
Isabel: I'm still an outsider, a foreigner. I need to ask all kinds of questions about all kinds of things that California natives take for granted. But I

must say that after the September 11 terrorist attack I feel much more at home. I feel that now I am an American. General Pinochet's military coup also took place on September 11 – the very same date. It, too, was a terrorist attack on a democratic country.

Jonah: Will you write something about or inspired by the terrorist attacks on the United States?

Isabel: I don't know. It's too soon to tell. I need distance. A novel always takes time. I have to internalize the experience and live it inside before I can write about it.

Jonah: How do you feel about curtailing civil liberties in order to combat terrorism?

Isabel: It's unavoidable. Life has changed forever. If we want more security we'll have to have less liberty. All over the world people feel increasingly unsafe. All over the world people have been living for decades with the fear of terrorist attacks. Now that same fear is here. Americans are experiencing what the rest of the world has long known and lived with. But the terrorist attack of September 11, 2001 is not the end of the world. We can not let it be the end of the world.

Jonah: Have you talked to people in Chile about it?

Isabel: Yes. There's a ripple effect. Chile is hurting. People there feel the terror, and there's an economic recession in Chile, too.

Jonah: Is your mother still your very first reader?

Isabel: She's a fierce critic. If my mother likes a book, the critics will like it, too. She likes *Portrait in Sepia* and so I feel safe.

Jonah: What are you writing now?

Isabel: A small book for the *National Geographic*, a book about nostalgia and the sense of place. I have been a wandering pilgrim. I don't have roots in any one geographical place. My roots are in my own memory and in my books.

Jonah: Are you going on the road to promote *Portrait in Sepia*?

Isabel: I'll be traveling around America, but my European trip had to be canceled. I was supposed to leave on September 12, and of course there were no flights. The tour has been rescheduled for next year.

Jonah: What do you miss most about Chile?

Isabel: The sense of a large extended family, the sense of belonging to a common history, of being bound by unbreakable things. I have created a fake family here, a kind of tribe, but it's mostly made up of friends, not blood relations. When I saw the movie, *The Godfather,* I knew the feeling it conveys about family. I said, "I could be the Godfather."

Jonah: Is your writing shaped or influenced by the book culture of northern California?

Isabel: No, I live in a secluded way. I have a few friends who are writers, but I'm not a group person. The fact that I still write in Spanish isolates me even more. Other writers I know share their manuscripts. I don't do that. For me, writing is such a solitary pursuit. As an author, I'm always alone.

Bill Barich

Carson Valley

In *Big Dreams* (1994), a gripping narrative of his own intense journey across California, Bill Barich described everything about the Golden State, from the past to the present and from Oregon to the Mexican border. *Carson Valley*, a novel, isn't quite as expansive. Set in the present day, right here in our own Sonoma County, in fact, it couldn't be closer to home, or more deeply embedded in local culture, especially local viticulture. *Carson Valley* holds a mirror up to town and vineyard, to newcomers and old-timers, and helps us to see ourselves as individuals and as a community.

Some readers have suggested that *Carson Valley* recalls John Steinbeck's fiction, and there are some obvious similarities. But to me, Barich's novel has far more in common with those big 19th-century novels that cover the canvas of a whole society at a particular moment in history. Indeed, *Carson Valley* seems more akin to George Eliot's *Middlemarch* (1872) than to *Grapes of Wrath* (1939) or *East of Eden* (1952). Like George Eliot, Barich is a literary realist rather than a symbolist or mythmaker. Like Eliot, his territory is mostly provincial rather than big city life, and his characters are mostly rural folk though there are a few high-powered New Yorkers in these pages.

Like Eliot, who created the fictional town of Middlemarch, Barich has created a fictional town and a fictional valley which he calls Carson. You won't find either the town or the valley on any map or in any atlas of Sonoma County, but it's as palpable as anyplace on the face of the earth. It has its own newspaper, of course, the ubiquitous *Valley Herald*, its social events and its gossip, its misfits and conformists.

As in most novels that capture the sweep of an entire society, *Carson Valley* offers a diverse cast of characters, most of them grouped around Victor Torelli, an old and very charming Italian farmer who reminds me of some of my neighbors in Sebastopol. There's Victor's free-spirited daughter Anna, his ranch foreman Arthur Atwater, and his main field worker, Antonio Lopez, who has a wife and a family of his own. In

addition, there's Torelli's wife Claire who dies of cancer, his laid-back son
Roger, who grows marijuana in Mendocino County and works part-time as
a cook in a vegetarian restaurant, and his old friends who serve as a kind
of Greek chorus, commenting on people and events.

Barich's diverse cast of characters enables him to explore the
interactions, the clashes and the conjunctions between social classes and
ethnic groups: Anglos and Latinos, yuppies and laborers. The novel
follows one year in the life of Torelli's vineyards, from bleak winter and
bright spring to glorious summer and the grape harvest in autumn. At the
end we're back in winter, but nothing is quite the same as it was, not in the
lives of the main characters, or in the life of the community either. There's
more gentrification, more suburbs, more corporate, as opposed to family
owned and operated, vineyards and wineries.

At the heart of this novel – and this is a novel with lots of heart –
are Arthur Atwater and Anna Torelli, both of whom are recently divorced,
distrustful of romantic love and domestic life, and both of whom don't
conform to the rigid social code of the valley. As one might imagine,
Arthur and Anna fall in love, the kind of love that middle-aged people
often think is no longer possible. Barich describes their passion and heart-
break and devotion in such loving detail, and with such compassion that
one can't help but identify with both of them, and live vicariously through
their emotional ups and downs. And then there's the sex. The scenes of
Arthur and Anna making love are too brief, at least for my taste, but
they're vivid, tender, erotic. I can't think of a contemporary novel that has
more evocative descriptions of two adults making love.

Carson Valley made me cry as I've rarely cried before, at least not
for a long, long time. It also made me smile, chuckle and laugh out loud as
I've rarely laughed before. Barich's novel is very funny, very sad, very
searing and very, very healing. There are so many wonderful scenes, so
many delightful details – Claire Torelli's funeral, Antonio Lopez's meditation on the face of President Jackson, which graces the $20 bill in his
wallet, Arthur and Anna's canoe trip down the Russian River, and the
rebellion of the field workers, to name just a few. The form of the novel is
also pleasing. There's a sense of aesthetic balance that's normally associated with the English novel, rather than with rough-and-tumble American
fiction.

One day in the not-too-distant future, *Carson Valley* will undoubtedly find its way to reading lists in courses on California literature. Graduate students at colleges and universities will write dissertations about it. They'll call *Carson Valley* a bicoastal love story, an agricultural epic, a novel that celebrates ethnic identity. Moreover, they'll dissect Barich's poetic prose, exhume his metaphors, and show how he expands the boundaries of California fiction, shattering stereotypes and clichés (there are no earthquakes here and no hot tubs, either) to create a sophisticated and intricate portrait of a provincial yet universal place.

Meanwhile, this is a novel to be savored, a novel to be enjoyed. Barich's *Carson Valley* has the power to make you laugh, to make you cry, to break your heart, and then to make you feel new and whole all over again. It is a major work of American fiction by a major contemporary California author, a novel about Sonoma County that captures our place and our time, not just for us, but for everyone, from coast to coast, from sea to shining sea.

Bill Barich: Notes from a Native Son

Bill Barich has always had a strong sense of place, whether it's Long Island, where he was born and raised, or San Francisco, where he settled in the early 70s. But probably no place has been as important to him as the Alexander Valley in Sonoma County, where he and his wife lived in a trailer from 1976 to 1981.

"Those five years in Sonoma County were really important to me," Barich says during a recent phone conversation from his home in Marin County. "I lived an isolated life, and that isolation forced me to listen not only to the landscape, which I love, but to my own inner voice."

It took Barich just two years to write *Carson Valley*, but it was a lot longer in the making. "I began to make notes ten years ago," he says. "I was haunted by the landscape, and by the people I had come to know."

The rich material that informs the novel seemed impenetrable, until Barich had what he calls a "lucky break." One morning he sat down and wrote a description of Victor Torelli watching an X-rated video in his office – which turned out to be the opening scene in the novel – and from then on there was no stopping him.

There's no X-rated sex in *Carson Valley*, but the sexual scenes between Torelli's daughter Anna and Arthur Atwater are definitely erotic. "It's hard to write about sex and not to pander," Barich says. "But I think that it's easier to write about sex now then it was when I was a kid growing up in the fifties. Writing about sex isn't the earthshaking thing it once was. We've had D.H. Lawrence, and nowadays kids can rent X-rated videos almost everywhere."

Bill Barich seems to have much in common with Arthur Atwater, the hard-working, passionate hero of the novel, and though we see *Carson Valley* through his point of view, we also watch him and the world around him from Anna Torelli's perspective. "It was liberating to write from a woman's point of view," Barich says. "When I sat down to write about Anna and Arthur, I played back old tapes of things that women had said to me. I thought about my relationships to women, and about my friends' relationships, too."

When he writes non-fiction, Barich says that the challenge is to animate the details, and that when he's writing fiction the challenge is to make it real. Having lived in Sonoma County seems to have made it possible for him to describe Carson Valley as though it really does exist. "The town of Carson Valley is drawn from many different towns," he says. "It's a bit of Healdsburg, and Guerneville and Sonoma, too."

Recently, Barich returned to the Alexander Valley to go fishing and to revisit native soil. "It's really not all that changed," he says. "It still stands as a kind of paradise. I don't know what you could want that's not there. I miss it. I miss being close to the land, and tied to the seasons. God bless the grapes! If it weren't for the grapes, it would be all bungalows, just like Long Island from which I escaped."

Amy Tan

The Bonesetter's Daughter

The Bonesetter's Daughter, Amy Tan's fourth novel, is about healers and healing – bonesetters - and it's about the ways that mothers are set in the very bones of their daughters. "A mother is always the beginning," one of the characters proclaims. Not surprisingly the novel begins with a mother and ends with a mother, too. In fact, it ends with the word "mother." There's no other way that it could end and still be true to itself.

Part comedy of manners, part historical epic, *The Bonesetter's Daughter* follows the lives of three independent women across the centuries. There's Gu Liu Xin, the daughter of the bonesetter – the doctor – in a Chinese village not far from Peking, in the last days of the emperor. Then there's Gu's daughter LuLing Liu Young, who comes of age during the war with the Japanese and who leaves China for America in the late 1940s. Finally, there's Gu's granddaughter Ruth who is born and raised in San Francisco and whom we meet in the late 1990s when she's in the midst of a mid-life crisis.

Ruth will be the most familiar of the women characters – to Western readers. Growing up, she has all the anxieties of the awkward American teenage girl and Tan describes those anxieties to perfection. Like many teenage girls, Ruth wants to fit in and to be like everyone else in her class. "I'm an American," she tells her mother. "I have a right to privacy, to pursue my own happiness." She does pursue her own happiness, but as she matures she comes to realize that she's deeply Chinese and that means that her mother's happiness counts as much as her own.

As a young woman, Ruth graduates from college, gets married and then divorced. Then she becomes romantically involved with Art Kamen who is Jewish and who has two daughters from a previous marriage. Ruth's section of the novel is the funniest, and Tan delights in making good-hearted fun of yoga classes, self-help books, and all sorts of New Age notions. Ruth insists that stress is her "preferred form of exercise." She's a doctor of sorts – a book doctor and ghost writer, and she turns out one pop psychology book after the next, most of them with cute titles like

Righting the Wronged Child.

Some of the scenes in this section seem predictable – like the wild meal with all the members of the cross-cultural family in a busy Chinese restaurant. Still it's fun to watch and listen to the Chinese characters and the Jewish characters eating eggplant with fresh basil, and a clay pot dish of meatballs and rice vermicelli. It's a scene ready-made for the movies.

The least familiar scenes of the novel take place in China, from the time of World War I to the end of World War II – as the Chinese Communist Party takes control of the whole country. Historical events – civil wars, guerrilla wars and massacres – provide an epic backdrop for a heart-wrenching family chronicle that's mostly set in Immortal Heart Village – home to the bonesetter's ancestors for more than 600 years.

Tan is terrific at conveying a sense of the big social and political transformations without sacrificing the nuances of personal identity, and the drama of the human heart. If you want a sense of how the lives of Chinese women changed over the course of the 20th century, then by all means read *The Bonesetter's Daughter*. There's hardship and adversity, but the mothers and their daughters never give up – even when they are widows and orphans. You finish the novel and you feel that for the Chinese there really has been genuine liberation over the past one hundred years.

The Bonesetter's Daughter doesn't develop chronologically or proceed in a linear fashion. It's built like a rare old Chinese box with boxes inside boxes inside boxes. Here there are stories inside stories inside stories. Open one story and it leads to another and another. But no matter where you open the book, you find the same stormy conflicts between mothers and daughters. If Tan's young women rebel against their mothers – if they lie to them and even hurt them – they are in the end their mother's faithful daughters. Even in New Age California, they retain ancient Chinese traditions.

All the main characters are storytellers, and all of them are keepers of the family secrets. Moreover, they read one another's stories, and it's the act of reading – as well as the act of writing – that gives the women characters a sense of their own identity, dignity and their rightful place in the world.

There's a lot that goes on in this novel – including the art of translation, and translation becomes a metaphor in its own right. The daughters continually translate for their mothers – from English to Chinese and from the ways of America to the ways of the old country. And so if *The Bonesetter's Daughter* is about the healing that takes place between mothers, daughters and granddaughters, it's also about the magic power of translation across generations, continents and cultures. Near the end of the novel, Ruth comes to the fearful and yet comforting discovery that she is "her mother's child and mother to the child her mother had become." It's the last ironical twist in a novel instilled with a sense of irony.

Do you have to be a mother or a daughter to love this novel? Absolutely not! Matriarchal values may be embedded in the very fabric of Tan's Chinese tale, but *The Bonesetter's Daughter* is for men, too, for sons, brothers and fathers. After all, our mothers are in our bones, too.

Amy Tan: Home, Books and Her First Publication

The Bonesetter's Daughter, Amy Tan's fourth novel, has been on *The New York Times Book Review* bestseller list for months. Tan herself has been on a turbulent 20-city book tour that has taken her from coast-to-coast, and to all sorts of places in between: Iowa City, Iowa; Oxford, Mississippi; Birmingham, Alabama; and Memphis, Tennessee. Arranging for a half-hour phone interview took weeks, but I finally caught up with Tan one morning when she was in between airplane flights and bookstore appearances.

Jonah: So you're at the Four Seasons in Palm Springs, Florida now.
Amy: Yes, I can see the Atlantic Ocean from the hotel window.
Jonah: How is the tour going?
Amy: I've been on tours as long as this one, but nothing as grueling; it seems to get harder each time. I'm not as young as I used to be and traveling on airplanes is terrible. I'm supposed to go to the UK and Australia next, but I'd like to get out of that last leg.
Jonah: You were born in Oakland, California in 1952, and you live now in both San Francisco and New York. What do you think of as home?
Amy: San Francisco, in my orange bedroom. I painted it orange so I'd know I was at home when I woke in the morning and opened my eyes. There's no other bedroom in the world that has that color orange.
Jonah: *The Bonesetter's Daughter* is in part about memory and so I wonder what memories you have of growing up in Santa Rosa in the early

1960s?

Amy: I lived in Santa Rosa when I was in the third, the fourth and part of the fifth grade. We lived in a house on the corner of Sacramento and Sartori. I went to Matanzas Elementary School – my teachers were named Grutoff, Foster and Stark. Miss Grutoff was wonderful. I learned the whole multiplication table in just a week, so she gave me paper and crayons and let me sit in a corner and draw pictures. I loved it.

Jonah: What did you read as a child?

Amy: Girls' books. I read all the Laura Ingalls Wilder books – *Little House on the Prairie*, *Little House in the Big Woods*.

Jonah: Did you read about China or the Chinese?

Amy: I read books about missionaries in China. I think they influenced me when I was writing the section of *The Bonesetter's Daughter* that describes the missionary school for girls. There was also a book about the monkey king that I lost long ago and would like to find.

Jonah: What about Pearl Buck, the author who interpreted China for several generations of Americans?

Amy: I read *The Good Earth*, of course, but not until much later in life.

Jonah: Your very first publication was in *The Press Democrat*.

Amy: Yes, it was an essay in a contest sponsored by the Citizen's Committee for the Santa Rosa Library. I was only eight years old. I think I won because I ended the essay by saying I was giving my savings to the Committee – all 18 cents of it. I won first prize – a transistor radio. I thank *The Press Democrat* for launching my literary career.

Jonah: In that essay, "What the Library Means to Me," you wrote, "I love school because the many things I learn seem to turn on a light in the little room in my mind." Metaphor seems to have come naturally to you, as though you were a born writer.

Amy: Maybe so. I do wonder at what age children begin to think in terms of metaphor. It would be fascinating to discover that. My father was a minister and he'd read his sermons to me. He used lots of metaphors, so maybe I was influenced by him.

Jonah: In your books you've mostly written about your mother, but your father was an important figure in your life, too, wasn't he?

Amy: He was an engineer. When we lived in Santa Rosa he had a job in Forestville, and he was also the assistant pastor of the Baptist Church. I think it was mostly an honorary position, and didn't pay.

Jonah: You've made major discoveries about your mother's past and her side of the family. All sorts of secrets – like your mother's real name – have come to light. What about your father's side?

Amy: I don't know a lot about my father's family, though I do know that my Tan grandfather was a Presbyterian minister in China. He learned to read and write in English before he learned to read and write in Chinese, though Chinese was his first spoken language. My father was one of 12 kids; all of them grew up to be evangelical ministers and missionaries. They traveled all over China stumping for Jesus.

Jonah: And you were raised a Baptist in Santa Rosa?

Amy: Absolutely! I went to church on Sunday and to Bible summer school. I had perfect attendance, and I memorized long passages from the Bible and earned extra credit for that.

Jonah: You finished an entire draft of your novel, *The Bonesetter's Daughter*, and then after your mother died you rewrote the whole book, didn't you?

Amy: When I was writing the novel I was in the midst of losing two people I loved very much – my mother and my editor Faith Sale – so I couldn't see the story clearly. I didn't know that the book I was writing was about loss. I felt like I was in the middle of the ocean. Later, I felt like I was on shore, and I knew I wasn't drowning, so I could go back and write the book in a different way.

Jonah: What's different about the published version of *The Bonesetter's Daughter*?

Amy: In the first draft there was nothing about the archeological excavations for Peking Man that took place in China in the 1920s. And the first chapter which is entitled "Truth," and which is a kind of Prologue to the novel, didn't exist at all in the original. I didn't write it until I was almost finished with the book.

Jonah: The first sentence of the book is "These are the things I know are true."

Amy: It wasn't the original first sentence.

Jonah: Did you do research to write the book?

Amy: I read old *National Geographic* magazines about China. And I did research about what China was like during the war with the Japanese in the 1940s. On one trip I made to China I met the man who led the archeological work in 1929 – he was about 100 – and talking to him helped write the section about Peking Man.

Jonah: Do you read or speak Chinese?

Amy: I speak children's Mandarin. I can gossip with my sisters, and order food in a restaurant, but I can't have an intellectual conversation.

Jonah: *The Bonesetter's Daughter* has been widely reviewed and enthusiastically praised.

Amy: I haven't read the reviews. My publishers gave me a folder of them when I arrived here, but I just threw them away. And interviews with me just make me feel self-conscious and strange, so I don't read them anymore, either.

Jonah: What have you learned about your own readers on this trip?

Amy: I meet a lot of mothers and daughters, of course, and recently I've been meeting people who have lost or are in danger of losing a parent. It's been a moving experience to hear their stories.

Robin Beeman

A Minus Tide

The novella is a tough form that gives trouble to even the toughest of writers. Longer than a short story and shorter than a novel, it adheres to its own literary conventions, and yet it shares common ground with both the novel and the short story. Those who know how to exploit it for all it's worth – like Jim Harrison, the author of *Legends of the Fall*, and *The Woman Lit By Fireflies* – have turned out contemporary masterworks.

Robin Beeman, who lives in Occidental and teaches creative writing at Sonoma State University, already has a collection of short stories – *A Parallel Life* – to her credit, and she's said that she would like to write a novel next.

A Minus Tide, her novella, is a step in that direction, a short and in some ways simple book that has a large cast of complex characters. At 91 pages it's just the right length to read in a single, comfortable sitting, and to become swept-up in its somber mood.

Chapter one of the novella describes a stand of Douglas fir that's cut down because it threatens a house and the novella's main characters – Evan and Mattie. Once the stand is gone there's more light, but there's also a sense of loss – as though there's a hole in the sky. The book ends where it begins, with an image of the place where the firs once dominated the landscape. "Beyond the window where the trees had stood I saw a vast emptiness," Mattie says. "I would never have predicted how once so much could be there and now not be there at all."

A Minus Tide is set somewhere along the coast of northern California, sometime near the present. It might be Jenner, Gualala, Mendocino or Casper and it could be just as recently as yesterday. As one might expect, it's about a loss in the human as well as in the natural environment. Sally, a folk singer, world traveler and lost soul, dies when her Toyota veers off the highway and into the Pacific Ocean, leaving her family, her friends and her lovers feeling there's a tear in the fabric of their lives. Whether Sally's death is an accident – the road is dangerous – or a suicide is not clear and the ambiguity heightens the effect. One of the many pleasures of Beeman's book is that it leaves you wondering what might have been going on in Sally's mind before her fatal plunge, and what part the people around her played in her death. Clearly no one is guilty of murder, but there's an abiding sense that most if not all the characters are in some way culpable – that there's been a collective failure on the part of the community to prevent one of its members from literally going over the edge.

The tangled lives of the main characters – Sally's older sister Mattie, and Mattie's husband Evan, as well as Joel and Anna – are revealed in the wake of Sally's death. ("a minus tide," we're informed, is an exceptionally low tide that exposes things that are usually covered up.) Beeman says a lot in a relatively short space; she compresses the histories of her main characters, especially their attachments of the heart.

Much of the book is lyrical, poetical. Beeman writes with a strong sense of place, of wooded hills, isolated ridges and a rugged coastline. And she writes especially well about the characters she seems to know inside and out as though they're among her closest friends.

Mattie, my favorite character, is an artist and a college teacher who has had a passionate affair in Italy that she hasn't recovered from, or from the death of her lover. Joel is also compelling – a lusty criminal lawyer with a wife and children. All the main characters take turns telling this moral tale so we get to see Sally in the round and to understand her more fully.

When I closed the book, I wished that it had been longer and that I could have spent more time watching the lives of the characters unfold over the years. I wanted Evan and Mattie to inhabit a full-fledged novel, not a novella. I wanted to feel that I was lodged inside their heads, to see the world more fully through their eyes and to listen to their voices at greater length. Still, I came away from *A Minus Tide* feeling that it was a plus for Beeman and for her readers. The story left me with a sense that after betrayal, forgiveness is possible, that love can be reborn and that relationships can start anew.

Robin Beeman: Literary Hybrid

Robin Beeman speaks with a sense of pride about her Southern roots and heritage, and especially her birth in New Orleans. But exactly when she was born, she's not eager to say. Borrowing an expression she heard first from her own mother, she explains, "I'm as old as my tongue and a little older than my teeth."

When she was a young girl, Beeman moved, with her mother and father, from New Orleans a short distance north to Covington in Saint Tammany Parish. The town boasted one famous writer – Walker Percy, the author of *The Movie Goer*, among other books.

"Percy was a gentleman writer, and he was fun to talk to," Beeman says. "He was always writing something and he always had opinions about writing, too. He liked to share his opinions with me, even when I was 11 or 12, and I enjoyed listening to him. From an early age I understood that there were people who loved to write."

As a teenager, Beeman left home and went into the wide, wide world. For a while, she lived and attended college in Mexico. Then, in the early 1970s, she settled in Sonoma County – first in Camp Meeker, later in Occidental. She's been here ever since, though she spent a year at the Iowa Writer's Workshop, where she received an MFA.

"California is a beautiful and an exciting place to live," she says. "I always feel like I'm on the edge here. In California, it's freer than in Louisiana and it's always exhilarating, but I'm not sure that it's a great place to write. Here, everything is always changing and for newcomers like me it's not clear what the rules are. In Louisiana, there's an oral tradition. Everywhere you turn all kinds of people tell stories with the intent of sucking you in and entertaining you."

Beeman remembers that her own mother filled notebooks with anecdotes and tales – and never published a single word. She remembers, too, that her father was one of the best storytellers in Covington – a town known for its storytellers. There's a tinge of nostalgia in her voice when she talks about life in Covington. After all these years, there's still a lot of the South in Beeman and perhaps there's something Southern about her short stories and her novellas, too, though all her characters are Californians. You might call her a literary hybrid.

Now and then, Beeman goes back to Louisiana. Occasionally, she thinks she'll buy a place of her own and spend part of each year in Saint Tammany Parish. But she hasn't made a move yet. "Occidental is at the center of my universe," she says. "This is home. I love it here. The old families are very good to tolerate outsiders like me in their midst."

Alexander Saxton

Bright Web in the Darkness

Long, long ago – long before Alan Greenspan, Nasdaq, and the World Trade Organization – the nation was in the grip of the Great Depression, and Americans were far worse off economically than they have been ever since. It was the 1930s and millions of men and women were unemployed. There was hunger, homelessness and talk of class warfare in the streets. Best-selling writers like John Dos Passos, John Steinbeck and Mike Gold wrote about workers, trade unions and militant strikes. Literature was supposed to be a weapon in the class struggle.

Alexander Saxton – who lives in Santa Rosa and who is probably the oldest living novelist in Sonoma County – came of age in that tumultuous era. Now 81 years old, he is retired after teaching American history – and writing about American history, too – for more than twenty years at UCLA. (He may also be the oldest living author of history books in the county.) Today, he is still writing and still living a vigorous life. Moreover, he is enjoying a revival as a novelist of the American working class.

Over a fifteen year period – from 1943 to 1958 – Saxton published three proletarian novels – *Grand Crossing*, which I first read as a boy, *The Great Midland,* and *Bright Web in the Darkness*. Unfortunately, *Grand Crossing*, which is largely autobiographical, remains out of print. *The Great Midland* has been reissued by the University of Illinois Press. *Bright Web in the Darkness*, which takes place both on the home front and overseas during World War II, has been reissued by the University of California Press with an eloquent essay by Tillie Olsen. *Bright Web* is probably Saxton's most polished novel. It is also probably the most accessible of his novels, and perhaps more so than when it was first published in 1958, when it struck some readers as a curious cultural relic of a bygone historical era: a paean to the proletariat.

Now, nearly 45 years later, it is enjoying a second life. For those who like to get a sense of the past from historical novels rather than from history books this novel is exemplary. Saxton's novel conjures the feeling of what it was like to toil in the shipyards of the Bay Area during World

War II, and what it was like to serve in the Merchant Marine during that era. Oddly enough, *Bright Web* turns out to be much more than a proletarian novel from the polemical past. Indeed, you might want to read it for what it has to say about love, marriage and friendship – themes that transcend the class struggle. I found myself as intrigued by the personal relationships between the main characters, as I was by the overtly political threads of the book.

What's also surprising here is that the main character, Joyce Allen, is a young African-American woman making her way as a welder and as a pianist in the awesome white world of San Francisco. So *Bright Web* turns out to be as much about art and ethnicity (and sexuality, too) as it is about class and class consciousness. It isn't only Marxist. I can't imagine many white male novelists today writing about a black, working class woman, but that's what Saxton did in the 1950s, and he succeeds remarkably well in making Joyce Allen a complex character.

Stylistically, the novel blends literary realism with a kind of poetic impressionism. What makes the writing memorable, page after page, are Saxton's indelible images of light and dark, especially the image of the "bright web in the darkness," which suggests that art proffers salvation for humanity. "The bright web in the darkness, the heart singing like a violin string," Joyce thinks as she listens to music. "The speck of foam on the wave, the tatter of cloud across the desert sky."

Alexander Saxton: Act I to Act IV

Alexander Saxton has reinvented himself again and again. He's been a carpenter, a teacher – mostly at UCLA – a writer, an historian, an organizer for the Longshoremen's Union and from 1941 to about 1960 a member of the American Communist Party. In hindsight he's critical of The Party but neither apologetic nor ashamed of his participation. "The worst aspect of the American CP was its failure to understand what was happening in Russia under Stalin," he says. "The best of the CP was its commitment to battle racism and to democratize the labor movement." In the late 1950s he was called to testify before the House Committee on Un-American Activities – better known as HUAC. "The Committee asked me to name names," he says. "I took the Fifth Amendment. I didn't want to testify about anyone I'd known and I didn't want to denounce anyone."

Saxton was born in 1919 and grew up in Manhattan on East 18th Street near Third Avenue. His parents were middle class and voted Democratic. They were also literary and bookish: Saxton's mother taught high school English – she also advocated equal rights for women; his father worked as an editor at *Harper's* and it was through his father that Alex met Edna St. Vincent Millay, John Dos Passos and other writers of the period. As a young man, he was influenced by the radical literature of the 1930s, especially the novels of Dos Passos. He was also radicalized by the social and political upheavals of the decade: the Depression, the Spanish Civil War, the Scottsboro Case and the rise of the Congress of Industrial Organizations – the CIO. His first novel, *Grand Crossing*, is about a young man not unlike himself – a young man from a well-off family who joins the working class.

For two-and-a-half years, Saxton attended Harvard. Then he "just left," as he puts it. He completed his college education at the University of Chicago. During World War II, he served in the Merchant Marine and after the war, he settled with his wife Trudy, whom he had married in 1941, in Sausalito.

"In those days the Bay Area was unique," he says. "More unique than it is now. The Longshoremen's Union really changed the culture of the whole area. It provided a labor base for a left-orientated political and artistic literary culture, which flourished in the 1930s and 1940s and continued to be influential until the 1970s." For years Saxton worked as a construction carpenter. "I had the option of moving up in the building trades," he says. "But I didn't want to become a contractor. I liked being a carpenter."

It was while he was working as a carpenter that he wrote *Bright Web in the Darkness*, about the shipyards of the Bay Area and its workers. "I wrote it on rainy days in winter and on weekends," he says. "I wrote it whenever I had a spare moment."

Bright Web was published in 1958 and though there were good reviews and modest sales, Saxton hasn't published a novel since then. "I gave up writing novels," he says. "It was impossible to earn a living." But he never stopped writing. In 1971 he published *The Indispensable Enemy: Labor and the Anti-Chinese Movement in California*, and in 1990, *The Rise and Fall of the White Republic: Class, Politics and Mass Culture in*

Nineteenth-Century America.

"I'm in Act Four of my life now," he says. "I'm also still in Act One, Scene One. In some ways I'm very different than I was as a young man, and in some ways I'm still the same. At 20, I thought that all good ideas would come from the working class and that the salvation of humanity would come from the exploited classes. I have modified that view. But I still think that capitalism is horribly destructive, and I still think that we have to have an economic system with far less lethal competition. We have to end the cycle of exploited classes coming to the top and exploiting other classes."

Michael Chiarello

Napa Stories:
Profiles, Reflections and Recipes from the Napa Valley
with Janet Fletcher, photographs by Steven Rothfeld

There are boatloads of cookbooks – books by cooks with recipes for roasts, ragus and rhubarb pies. And then there are cook's books – those uncommon books by cooks that explore all sorts of subjects, from exotic foods to far-away places. Michael Chiarello's *Napa Stories* is both. It has stunning recipes, and vibrant stories about real people, real places and really delicious food. It's a big, beautiful coffee table book with dozens of gorgeous color photos by Steven Rothfeld that capture the contours of Napa County, and the familiar faces of its celebrated winemakers, including Robert Mondavi and Joseph Phelps. Turning the pages of this book you think Napa is the nexus. Why venture to Tuscany, the author seems to say, when rustic, romantic Napa is right next door?

The recipes may be the best part of the book. For years Chiarello was an innovative chef – at Tra Vigne, his starship restaurant in St. Helena. More recently, he's set up shop on PBS television; his current show, *Michael Chiarello's Napa* is broadcast on 174 stations all across the country. Chiarello is an expert with a knack for making cooking contagious – all of which is to say that I love his recipes! Among my favorites are the braised rabbit crostini, the angry lobster with white beans, the frito misto – calamari fried in batter made from arborio rice and semolina – and the Bing cherry compote with basil gelato. Just reading about these dishes makes me want to cook and eat and eat and eat. I also love Chiarello's helpful hints. "The bigger the chicken the better the broth," he explains in a recipe for cappelletti in hen brodo with wild mustard greens. And, in a recipe for wine braised short ribs, he suggests that the secret is to soak the meat in a mixture of water, sugar, salt, juniper berries and bay leaves. The ribs turn out tender and they look great, too.

The recipe for gnocchi with mushroom sugo – a sauce made with 13 different ingredients, including wild mushrooms, red wine and fresh peeled tomatoes– explains how to make the gnocchi light. Bake the potatoes, don't boil them, and cut back on the flour, Chiarello suggests. The recipe for roast chicken with fennel and sage provides easy-to-follow directions. The ingredients are clearly described, and there are enticing tales about the author's own experiences, like harvesting fennel in the fields.

Chiarello's personal touch is everywhere in this book, and there are glimpses of the author himself outside the kitchen as "an old hippie," a hunter, a fisherman and the father of three daughters. But mostly, Chiarello is in the background, and his flamboyant Napa friends are in the foreground. There are dukes and duchesses, lords and ladies in these pages, like Belle and Barney Rhodes – the proprietors of Bella Oaks Vineyard and the "founding mother and father of the Napa Valley," as the author calls them. "If America had royalty, Barney and Belle Rhodes would be the duke and duchess of Napa Valley," Chiarello writes. There are also ordinary folk, and down-to-earth people. Chiarello introduces readers to the immigrants from Mexico who do the bulk of the work in the vineyards – and to Napa's inventive farmers and entrepreneurs, like Amy Wend who raises goats, and Heath Benson who makes cheese.

Napa Stories offers something for everyone: history, architecture, landscape, viticulture and even the politics of the region. Chiarello is an advocate for agricultural preservation and the wine industry. "Without wineries, Napa Valley would be just another San Francisco suburb," he writes. I especially like the stories he tells about Prohibition – when wine making went on, despite the law – and the current revolution in wine that began in the 1960s and that hasn't let up yet. And I like the way that the author takes his readers through the vineyard seasons: from spring pruning to fall harvesting.

This is a book I'll consult in the weeks and months ahead. Chiarello's hearty minestra dellí orto is perfect for fall. And in the dead of winter I'll want to devour his rich, tasty grilled lamb loins. "Buon gusto!," as they say in Italy – and in Michael Chiarello's Napa.

Michael Chiarello: California's Calabrian Chef

Once upon a time, Michael Chiarello owned nearly half a dozen restaurants, from Tra Vigne and Tomatina in St. Helena to Ajax Tavern in

Aspen, and Bistecca in Scotsdale. Now, for the first time in decades, he finds himself without a restaurant where he can make his authentic polentas, pastas and pizzas. A chef without a restaurant sounds like a fish out of water – or a newspaper columnist without a column – but that's not how it looks or feels to Chiarello himself. "I don't need a restaurant right now," he says. "And I didn't really change my own life. I just followed my customers into their homes. That's where most of us want to be, especially after 9/11, which caused a great disruption all over the planet."

Chiarello's first home was in Red Bluff, California in the Central Valley. He was born there on January 26, 1962, and reared in Turlock, in an Italian-American family with roots in Calabria, Italy. Perhaps if he'd been born in another generation he'd have stayed closer to home, but he went off bravely to the Culinary Institute of America (CIA) in Hyde Park, New York, and graduated in 1982 at the age of 20. For a few years, he worked in Florida. Then, in 1986, he became the chef at Tra Vigne, and over the next decade-and-a half he made his restaurant into a haven for local residents and a destination for tourists from all over the world. In 1995, the CIA named him Chef of the Year, and in 1998, he received the Robert Mondavi Culinary Award. For the last two years, he's been on TV and on radio. In fact, he's a man of all media. Chiarello has three books to his name, a website, and his own company, Napastyle, which boasts a glossy catalogue that offers customers everything from kitchen tools and coffee to napkins and dinnerware. Martha Stewart might well be envious.

This evening, shortly before Halloween, the charismatic Chiarello is cooking at Sur La Table – the kitchen store and more – on Maiden Lane in San Francisco, just off Union Square. A few dozen foodies have left their comfortable homes to watch him prepare a sumptuous four-course meal, and to eat each dish as it comes off the stove. I have a notepad and pencil balanced on one knee, and a plate with frito misto, the starter, on the other. For the next three hours, I'll watch Chiarello cook. I'll eat his food, listen to his stories and I'll go home feeling both well fed and emotionally nourished. I couldn't be happier.

The day before, I'd met Chiarello at Napastyle, his new company in St. Helena. We'd chatted for a couple of hours about bocce, grappa, gray salt, pecorino cheese, pesto, prosciutto, Sangiovese, semolina, vinegar, wild leeks and much, much more. At Sur La Table, I can see right away that Chiarello is a lot more flamboyant when he's on stage and in front of a large, lively audience. Indeed, he's a natural-born performer, raconteur, showman, comedian, and a passionate soapbox preacher, too, who advocates organic ingredients, living meaningful lives and cooking without fear.

Chiarello calls himself "a good Catholic boy," and indeed he talks about his mother with a sense of reverence and adoration. She's no longer alive, but she's still a powerful presence in his life, and still a strong influence on his style of cooking. At the same time, he's a bit of a wise guy. He brings out his Italian body language, and his Italian gestures when he needs to, and he explains that he enjoys *The Sopranos*, the HBO hit. "The show is brilliant," he says. "I watch it and I think, 'we're not like that,' and then I hear myself say, 'we're just like that.' In Calabria, there was more Mafia than in Sicily. That type of organization was put together to protect families. Good intentions were carried to extremes."

At Napastyle, Chiarello talked about well-stocked pantries, al dente pasta, shopping in North Beach with his mother when he was a boy, and about his years as a chef at Tra Vigne. "Restaurants are addictive," he said. "You start at 6:30 talking to the fish guy and then the produce guy. You work on what you'll showcase that day. At 11:30 the lunch customers arrive and that's a thrill. Then, suddenly it's the afternoon. You have a double espresso and you work on the evening meal. Then the dance for dinner begins. You talk to customers, invite them to try this or try that. You keep the excitement going. And the next day you do it all over again."

At Sur La Table, Chiarello is clearly stoked. "For most of my life I was a serious chef," he tells his audience. "Now I like to have fun in the kitchen." And, as though to prove his point, he uses the boot on his left foot as a prop to illustrate where Calabria is located on the boot of Italy. "My roots are here," he says. While he prepares the minestra delí orto, he does a charming imitation of Julia Child. Later, he pokes fun at Martha Stewart – "General Martha" he calls her – and the audience is in stitches. While we're eating the wine-braised short ribs with creamy polenta, he describes a $25,000-a-plate dinner – a fundraiser for Hilary Clinton – that he prepared at Steve Jobs's home. At the very end of the meal, while we're practically licking the Rombauer jam cake from our plates, Chiarello gets on his soapbox. He has recently returned from New York, and a visit to Ground Zero, and he's perhaps even more impassioned than ever before.

"It's good to be a patriotic American," he says. "But be patriotic to yourself, too. Celebrate yourself. Surround yourself with meaningful things. Life isn't just about buying. Take a day off. Take time to do nothing. Find someone old and ask them to tell you a story about their lives. When you cook, talk about the food you make and what it means to you."

Charles Rubin

4-F Blues:
A Novel of WWII Hollywood

The Hollywood novel – the novel about stars, starlets and studio moguls – is nearly as old as Hollywood itself. And yet like Hollywood, the Hollywood novel also manages to reinvent itself again and again – to bring audiences back for more entertainment. Indeed, there's nothing more entertaining than a suspenseful story about Hollywood that goes behind the scenes to show film stars stripped of their makeup, their props and their costumes.

Charles Rubin's *4-F Blues* borrows lock, stock and barrel from the genre of the Hollywood novel. If you've read literary classics like Budd Schulberg's *What Makes Sammy Run?* and F. Scott Fitzgerald's *The Last Tycoon,* you'll find echoes in these pages. Then, too, the author also takes what he needs from Hollywood films themselves – the gestures, the styles, and the costumes from the golden era of film – and that's part of the novel's unmistakable charm.

4-F Blues also breaks new ground and adds fresh and distinct ingredients to an old literary mix. Unlike Budd Schulberg and F. Scott Fitzgerald, Rubin excels as a comic author with a bizarre imagination. His novel is outrageously funny from beginning to end. If the characters and the situations that unfold don't provoke outright laughter and amusement they certainly tickle the funny bone. Sometimes the humor is subtle and sometimes it unfolds slowly. Slapstick and farce aren't the main attractions here, and *4-F Blues* doesn't offer a barrage of brilliant one-liners, either. Rubin's strength as a comedic writer is his ability to explore a big, bold concept – to beat it to death and then bring it back to life. Like many of the finest comedians, the author works best with deadly serious subjects, like German Fascism and the fate of American democracy itself.

The mad, mad, mad concept at the core of the novel is this: Nazi agents have infiltrated Hollywood from top to bottom and are doing their best to destroy it from within. (There are many movies, like Irwin Winkler's *Guilty by Suspicion*, and many memoirs, like Dalton Trumbo's

The Time of the Toad, about Communists in Hollywood, but *4-F Blues* seems to be the first work of fiction about Fascists in World War II Hollywood.) The time here is 1942, just after the bombing of Pearl Harbor, and the studios – Rubin's fictional production company is called Grove – are making pro-war pictures to please the White House, and to turn a tidy profit at the box office.

Moreover, it's a time when Hollywood's actresses are using their sex appeal to arouse patriotism on the home front and on the battlefield. The historical era is rich and complex, and Rubin exploits it for literary purposes. If there's a political message here, it's populist. In Rubin's casting, ordinary folk are the real stars of the American epic. A sense of nostalgia for the lost innocence and optimism of the early 1940s infuses *4-F Blues*.

It wouldn't be fair to the book or to the author to reveal the intricacies of the plot. But perhaps this much can be said. Marcus Woods and Vance Varley, two of the villains of the tale, are determined to kill Maggie Graym, Rubin's redheaded heroine, and thereby sabotage the film industry and undermine American morale. What Woods and Varley don't know is that Hitler himself is one of Graym's biggest fans, eager to keep her alive and on the silver screen. In one of the novel's early scenes – it's reminiscent of Charlie Chaplin's film *The Great Dictator* – Rubin describes Hitler as he watches one of Graym's pictures from the comfort of his own private screening room in Berlin. Rubin doesn't belittle the dangers of fascism, but he certainly pokes fun at der Fuhrer.

Like the heroines of Hollywood melodrama, Maggie Graym is almost always in danger and in distress, and like them she's rarely alone or undefended. Tom Driscoll, a movie stunt man who is 4-F – unfit for military duty – and his sidekick Douglas Tanaka, a Japanese teenager, rescue her again and again in the proverbial nick of time. There are extended chase scenes, of course, and edge-of-the-seat cliffhangers, too. Rubin pulls out all the stops. The clichés come fast and furious, and in this case the more the merrier. Real people collide with reel people – it's not always easy to tell them apart – good guys tangle with bad guys, and glamorous stars collide with common people.

Betty Davis has a cameo role and so does Humphrey Bogart. "Let go of the lady," Bogart tells a drunk and disorderly sergeant when he grabs Maggie Graym on the dance floor of the Hollywood Canteen, which provides the novel with its main setting. When Graym thanks Bogart for rescuing her, Rubin has him reply, "Don't think anything of it, kid." It's just what Bogart would have said in the movies, and maybe in real life, too – and it's the kind of playful touch that makes this novel a pleasure to read.

Charles Rubin: A (Serious) Stand-up Comedian

If it takes a worried man to sing a worried song, then it also takes a funny man to write a funny book. Charles Rubin – the author of several very funny books – *Hard Sell*, a satire of the advertising industry, and *Don't Let Your Kids Kill You*, a self-help book for parents with children on drugs – is a very funny man, indeed. Rubin's sense of humor is obvious from the moment he begins to talk about his own topsy-turvy life as a U.S. Marine during the War in Vietnam, as an advertising executive at BBDO – Batten, Barton, Durston and Osborne – and as a stand-up comedian in New York City, where he was born and where he was raised by two very funny parents.

"My mother was pure Lucille Ball," Rubin says, laughing. "She had an inherent sense of humor, and so did my father. Like them, I see humor in the human condition – and in tragedy. If I didn't, I'd have died a long time ago. Of course, my humor springs from my own experience. Whoever is feeding me my lines is probably Jewish. The stand-up comedy routine that I did for years was about a New Yorker who hates New York and who can't wait to get out of New York."

Nowadays, Rubin lives in a split-level house on the east side of Petaluma, a long, long way from the east side of Manhattan, where he began his romance with Hollywood movies. It's a rainy Saturday morning, and Rubin is sitting comfortably – he's wearing a dark blue sweater, dark slacks and sneakers – on the sofa in a large living room decorated with family photos and Chinese art.

"My brother Jackie and I were brought up in the dilapidated movie houses on Third Avenue," he explains. "MGM was our baby-sitter. As boys, we saw the same movies again and again. Going to the movies became a way of life. I suppose it's natural that I always wanted to write something about Hollywood."

Rubin has spent nearly a lifetime in the thrall of Hollywood movies

– mostly movies that were mauled by the media, or else obscure films that escaped the attention of reviewers. But he also enjoys the classics from the 1930s and the 1940s: John Huston's *The Maltese Falcon*, Alfred Hitchcock's *Sabotage* and, of course, *Casablanca*, probably the most delightfully patriotic picture that Hollywood has ever made. Oddly enough, Rubin finds himself in a town without a cinema to its name. "These days Petaluma doesn't have a single movie house," he says, rue-fully. "But then, I'm no longer a movie-goer, though I do watch movies on my VCR. For the most part, I'm disappointed by contemporary American movies, especially contemporary war movies. *Apocalypse Now* is humor-less, *Pearl Harbor* is a trite love story, and *Saving Private Ryan* didn't do it for me either, though I'm sure it educated kids who knew nothing about World War II."

Yes, Rubin sees humor in almost everything and everyone, includ-ing himself. "I'm a baby boomer," he says – and with the split-second timing of a veteran stand-up comedian – he adds, "a rapidly deteriorating baby boomer at that." Still he doesn't find much, if any, humor in war. "All wars are based on money," he says. "I never could laugh at Nazi concen-tration camps, or anti-Semitism, and bombs aren't one bit funny, either. All wars are idiotic."

Rebecca Solnit

Wanderlust: A History of Walking

I like to think that the history of walking in 20th-century America is encapsulated in my own family. For my grandfather walking and working were one and the same. A peddler, he carried a pack on his back and went door-to-door selling shoe laces, mirrors, shirts and more until he saved enough money to buy a store and didn't have to walk to make a dollar. My father walked to school in the small town where he was raised, went to college, became a lawyer, and when I was a boy made walking into a family regimen. When I grew up I walked as a way to escape from family, work and thinking. In unfamiliar cities – Madrid, Marrakech, Manchester – I walked to get out of my own skin and into another world.

Rebecca Solnit is also an habitual walker, and in *Wanderlust: A History of Walking* she recounts the pleasures and the pains of her own adventures on foot in San Francisco (where she lives), in London, Las Vegas and Paris, which she calls "a walker's paradise." The autobiographical anecdotes give this book a feeling of authenticity; we trust the author who has done the things she writes about. But *Wanderlust* is hardly a personal memoir about a life spent wandering at home and abroad. Indeed, what makes this book distinctive is that the author has read widely in the literature of walking, and thought deeply about the place of walking in history.

If I read her accurately, Solnit has two main points: first, walking has played a major part in defining and shaping our humanity; and second, the decline of walking reflects our alienation from the world around us and from our own selves. "We walk; therefore, we are," Solnit might say, as well as the corollary, "We don't walk; therefore, we lose our identity." Walking, she argues, puts us in touch with the earth and with our fellow human beings. For Solnit, walking goes hand in hand with public spaces, communal places and with a vibrant civic life; walking is democratic and egalitarian. The decline of walking, she insists, has gone hand in hand with anomie, paranoia, isolation. So walls and gates have gone up, and walking, which seems innocuous, has come to be regarded as subversive. And in some cities – one thinks of Los Angeles – walking is often regarded as insane.

Reading *Wanderlust* is like going on a brisk, though not a physically exhausting, walk. There are entertaining diversions along the way: the walkathon, the labyrinth, the treadmill. There's humor, playfulness and passionate engagement with ideas. This is intellectual and cultural history that makes an intimate connection to contemporary lives. I suppose my main complaint is that there isn't more to *Wanderlust*. So much has been written about walking, and walking has played such a significant part in human history, that it isn't possible to include all of it in a compact book. But Solnit has left out too much for my taste. She writes about walking in San Francisco, but says nothing about the gumshoe Sam Spade who walks across a landscape of crime and never does find the real Maltese falcon. There's no mention of Jack London's peripatetic novel *Valley of the Moon,* either.

Then, too, some of Solnit's comments sound glib. New York is a "masculine city," she insists and adds that "if cities are muses, it is no wonder this one's praises have been sung best by its gay poets." What about the heterosexual novelists – William Styron, Saul Bellow, E.L. Doctorow? Haven't they celebrated New York, made love to her in their work as much as the gay poets? I think so. I wish there had been more information about walking in America and about the American literature of walking on the wild side, so that the French, the English and the Germans didn't dominate these pages.

But Solnit certainly opens up the vast subject of walking for discussion and debate. She makes us aware of all the variations on travel by foot: marching, promenading, mountaineering, going on a pilgrimage. She invites us to look at walking and social classes, walking and sex, walking and politics, walking and religion. I know that when I go walking again I'll put one foot in front of the other as always, but somehow after reading this book I don't think that walking will ever be quite the same. *Wanderlust* made me feel more alive, more connected. It made me want to walk and talk, go nowhere in particular and make discoveries along the way.

Rebecca Solnit: "California is Like the Prow of the Ship"

She walks. She talks. She reads voraciously. And writes as though she's on fire. Rebecca Solnit hasn't yet celebrated her 40th birthday, but she has already published four provocative books: *A Book of Migrations, Savage Dreams, Secret Exhibition,* and most recently, *Wanderlust.* Together they make her one of the most versatile cultural historians in America today. Now she is writing a book about Silicon Valley, Hollywood and "the centrality of California to the global present."

Solnit wasn't born in California, but she moved here with her parents when she was an infant, and California, especially the Bay Area, has been central to her own genesis and evolution as an intellectual and an author. "California is like the prow of the ship," she says, energetically, during an early morning phone conversation from her home in San Francisco. "Californians get there first. The rest of the country follows us. Why is that? Maybe it's because we're so uprooted, so little grounded in tradition."

Solnit followed an unconventional path on her way to the life of the mind that she now enjoys outside academia. Raised on the "frontier of suburbia" in Novato, by parents she describes as "bookish and progressive," she never finished high school. After taking the equivalency exam she attended College of Marin for a year and then at 17 slipped away to Paris, where she studied at the American University. Next came San Francisco State and a graduate degree in journalism from UC Berkeley.

Walking was a part of Solnit's routine from the time she was a young girl growing up in Novato. To the south was the public library filled with books. "I wanted to be a ballet dancer until I learned how to read," she says. To the north were cow pastures and the rolling hills of Marin. "I have changed remarkably little since I was six or seven years old," she says.

Of course, walking still plays a big part in her life, whether it's in the city or in the country. "In San Francisco, I walk to the post office, the grocery store, the café, the bookstore," she says. "I'm usually solo. I do a lot of my thinking on foot. In the country walking is mostly recreational and in the company of others."

If she could have an ideal walking companion, who would it be? Solnit says that for walking on boulevards she would want to be in the company of Walter Benjamin, the German Jewish author who emerges as the secret hero of *Wanderlust*.

"I'd want William Wordsworth to take me over the moors, and John Muir to guide me through the wilderness," she says. "And I wouldn't mind having Virginia Woolf for company either. Her essay 'Street Haunting,' is the greatest essay on walking in the English language."

Watching San Francisco life has been one of Solnit's preoccupations for decades, and year after year she becomes more apprehensive. "The city's cultural diversity is under siege by the dotcoms," she says. "The people who sit at desks with computers are taking over. We're losing artists, dreamers, activists, walkers. It's like seeing a rain forest disappear."

Don Emblen

Want List
& Other Poems About Aging

You can't get more local on the literary scene than *Want List &
Other Poems About Aging*, available in paperback from Running Wolf
Press. The poems are by D. L. Emblen – known to his friends and col-
leagues as Don – the first ever Sonoma County Poet Laureate. The dra-
matic black-and-white blockprints in the book are by his wife, Linda
Emblen who also appears as a memorable figure in these pages. Moreover,
Chip Wendt, who is also a local poet and a longtime resident of
Healdsburg, designed and published the book.

One aspect of *Want List* that doesn't seem to be local is the lively
Introduction by William Booth, a native of Laporte, Minnesota. But Booth
might as well be from here; he certainly writes about Emblen's poems with
a keen sense of familiarity and appreciation. "Because he writes every day,
everyday life gets into the poems," Booth says. "The poems bring everyday moments up out of the everyday murk. That is what the awake imagination does – it rescues the 'ordinary' from oblivion." Yes, Emblen has
been rescuing and preserving and reaching out.

In fact, his sharply etched poems are not just local to Sonoma
County but to many other places, big and small, from here to Minnesota
and beyond. That's not surprising, since aging – the poet's theme – is as
far reaching as coming of age, or falling in love. As you'd expect, there are
poems here about old folks, old folks' homes, grandfathers, grandmothers,
dying and death. Mostly, these are poems that look back at life, poems in
which the author peers through a "rear view mirror" at a time and place
that is fast receding.

Again and again, Emblen seems to want us to see our familiar
world as though for the first time, all new and strange. In "Understanding
Your Aging Self," the reader is invited to "Lie down flat on your back./ Let
your eyes get used to seeing/ ceiling as ground, light bulbs as mushrooms." Here and elsewhere, Emblen's work is playful, practical and very
accessible. You can go deep into these poems, but there is almost always a

sense of immediate pleasure right on the surface, without digging or analyzing. And that's good news, of course, to those readers who often find that poems are difficult, obscure and inaccessible. *Want List* doesn't give you a chance to run away or hide. It grabs you, talks your language, enters your life.

Emblen is the sort of poet who travels one way and then can't help but travel the opposite way. And so if this volume is about aging, it is also about youth. There are poems about grandsons as well as grandfathers, and poems about the wild recklessness of young men as well as the disciplined rhythms of old men. In "Charters," there are images of "an old man in blue work clothes/ scything his field" and of "A boy on a motorcycle" who passes the poet in his car "insisting like a bullet: he must have his way." Emblen is also unpredictably pleasing; he doesn't always write in the exact same way. While there are poems that are born of the imagination there are also poems that derive from memory, and poems about the failing of memory. In "Where the Black Begins," the poet describes a teacher (perhaps himself) who "remains on his feet, as always,/ to keep the students on their toes," but who absentmindedly "forgets the title of the book he talks about."

In a few brief lines, Emblen creates memorable portraits of all sorts of people, including my favorite – the shoe shine man "with his flying elbows, wise-cracks,/ quick and rhythmic hands, his snapping cloth,/ the way he has when done/ of stepping back to see his work." There is probably a lot of that shoe shine man in Emblen himself, with his lyrical wise-cracks, and rhythmic hands and his own elbows flying when he's at work on his poems.

Want List strikes me as a book that enables the poet to step back and appraise his own work. And of course it enables readers to take yet another long, close look at the life-enhancing poetry of perhaps our most beloved local poet. (I say "perhaps" because as soon as you describe one poet as "most beloved" half-a-dozen other local poets leap up to say they are "most beloved.") Emblen has worked hard at his craft, but he has never elbowed his way to the forefront of the Sonoma County poetry world. His well-crafted poems speak for themselves, without fanfare, without drawing attention to the poet's own memory and imagination. But here now are a few last words from Emblen himself, who says that we "hear what we listen for," and who offers this wise plea: "If we but learn to listen/ to the crackle of persistent life."

Don Emblen: "The Puzzles of Writing Poetry"

Poets – especially poet laureates – aren't born in an instant or even in a long day, but slowly and steadily over time, like good poems or good wine. Don Emblen's career as a poet – and as Sonoma County's Poet Laureate – began more than 60 years ago with a woman named Alma Gunning. "It was Alma Gunning who introduced me to metaphor and to simile when I was a high school student," Emblen explains.

It's late afternoon in the library at the back of his house in Santa Rosa, and for a moment or two it seems as though Emblen might be a school boy again remembering his lessons. "Alma Gunning was a short, little, wispy woman, but she made a lasting impression on me," he says. "After I took her course I was hooked forever on figures of speech." But Emblen didn't dive head first into poetic language. At Los Angeles City College he took up the who, what, when, where, why and how of journalism. Then he went downtown to a job as a hard-nosed reporter, covering the police beat and the courts. When he wasn't writing the news, he was churning out novels and short stories, and now and then a poem or two.

During World War II, Emblen served as an officer in the Navy, and Alma Gunning's literary lessons began to grow on him slowly, steadily. "I wrote a lot of poems on a submarine chaser in the Pacific," he says. "It was a dinky ship and there was no privacy, but I made friends with the yeoman and he let me use his tiny cubicle. I wrote a whole volume in there – 100 poems or more – but not a single one of them was ever published."

After the war, Emblen went back to college on the G.I. Bill. By the late 1950s, he was teaching English at Santa Rosa Junior College, and his career as a poet took yet another turn. "I was trying to teach students to pay attention to figures of speech, to understand that they weren't just decorative," he says. "And teaching them taught me a lot about poetry." In the 1960s and 1970s he wrote hundreds of poems, but it wasn't until 1983, when SRJC published *Under the Oaks*, a collection of his work, that he finally went out on a limb (metaphorically speaking, of course), and called himself a poet. "I was doing all kinds of stuff before then," he says. "I was writing biography and publishing scholarly articles, and teaching, and I just didn't think that I'd done enough to call myself a poet. It took 50 years to get to that place."

Ever since then, there's been no stopping Emblen. By his own conservative estimate, he's written at least 4,000 poems, and they keep coming, at least twice a week. "This morning I went to Benzinger Winery to read my own poetry and talk about the literary scene in Sonoma County to a group of travel writers," he says. "When I got there, I was told they'd be an hour-and-a-half late. I might have fussed and fumed, but I sat down in the shade and started to work on a poem." Emblen doesn't know yet what the poem is about. So far all he has is an image that won't let him alone – an image of two identical, dead trees in an old, abandoned orchard. One tree is thick with noisy crows, the other doesn't have a single bird. "Why is that?" Emblen asks. "What do we make of it?" Sooner or later he'll know the answer, but he's not in any rush. The poem will take its own time being born, and that's probably the way his high school teacher Alma Gunning would want it.

After all these years, Emblen would rather write poetry than do almost anything else. And after all these years, poetry is still a challenge. "At 18, you write because you think it's exotic, or you think it makes you different, or you think it will make you better than other people," he says. "At 81, you don't care about being exotic, or even about the notoriety that comes from being the Sonoma County Poet Laureate. You write because you haven't figured everything out, because there's still something to learn, because you haven't solved all the puzzles of writing poetry."

Part III:
Private Eyes

Sarah Andrews

An Eye for Gold

By all the literary laws that have governed the hard-boiled school of murder mysteries, the detective has to be a solitary guy prowling the mean streets of Los Angeles or San Francisco. Whether he's Sam Spade in Dashiell Hammett's *The Maltese Falcon*, or Philip Marlow in Raymond Chandler's *The Big Sleep*, the private eye lives by a masculine code of honor that befits a hero on an epic quest in a land of evil. Not surprisingly, Spade and Marlow spawned dozens of look-alikes wearing fedoras, carrying guns – gats as they called them – and talking out of both sides of their mouths. They're still in our midst and yet increasingly the fictional detective today is likely to be a woman with distinctly feminine taste and sometimes an overtly feminist agenda.

Take the case of Sonoma County's Sarah Andrews, and the heroine of her murder mysteries who is a "daughter of the west." Unlike Spade and Marlow, Andrews's sleuth is far more at home in the wide-open spaces than she is in the labyrinth of cities. And unlike Spade and Marlow who rarely trust members of the opposite sex, her sleuth is likely to solve a case with a helping hand from another woman.

Andrews's detective is Emily Hansen – Em for short – and she has already appeared in five very lively and very entertaining novels including *Bone Hunter*, *Tensleep* and *Mother Nature*, which is set in Sebastopol – a few miles from the author's own home.

In *An Eye for Gold*, which is set mostly in the desert of Nevada, Hansen takes on a case that engages all her talents as a professional geologist and an amateur detective. Though she doesn't spout feminist manifestoes, she's an unattached, independent woman and very savvy about gender politics. Women readers will find her lovable and men will probably enjoy her spunk. Who wouldn't like a feisty, funny detective who drinks beer – micro-brewed of course – feasts on pizza and isn't afraid to wander from the well-beaten path? Part of the charm of *An Eye for Gold* is that Hansen's own story and her particular habits are revealed little by little as the mystery unfolds. Born and raised on a ranch in Wyoming,

Hansen has a knack for sizing up situations quickly and for reading the ways of strangers. She's ideal for detective work, though she's pulled into the art of tracking criminals against her own inclinations.

An Eye for Gold offers a panoramic view of Nevada's frontier society. It also presents compelling portraits of ornery Nevada folk: prospectors, prostitutes, scientists, squatters, miners and Indians. And of course, Andrews uses the novel as a vehicle to explore, survey and map the contours of the land itself. As the title suggests, *An Eye for Gold* is about gold – gold mining and gold fever – and the lengths to which men will go to acquire it. If you don't already know the history of gold in human affairs, this book provides much of the information you'd want.

The bodies pile up, the mystery deepens literally and figuratively – the clues eventually lead Hansen to an underground mine. There's suspense every step of the way and there are twists and turns that keep you turning the pages. *An Eye for Gold* also gives the reader food for thought. As a novel of ideas, it's intended to raise awareness about corporate greed, endangered species and consumer culpability in the depletion of natural resources.

"I have preferred in the Em Hansen books to present information rather than judgments, and have tried my best to continue in this book," Andrews says in the "Author's Note" at the back of the book. For the most part, she's good on her word. When it comes to her heroine, however, Andrews doesn't hesitate to take a clear stand. She's unambiguous about her support for Hansen. By the end of the novel, her heroine has two appealing offers – to join the FBI and to get married in the Mormon Church. Readers of the earlier novels may guess what choices she makes. But there are also plenty of surprises in store – even for old fans. If you haven't already met Hansen, it's time to make her acquaintance. If you've followed her adventures so far, you'll want to rejoin her as she investigates the immense spaces of the Great American West.

Sarah Andrews: The Hows and Whys of Her Whodunits

Recently I joined Sarah Andrews for breakfast in Graton – her hometown – and for an hour or so we talked intently about murder mysteries and about her own life. Born in Stamford, Connecticut, Andrews teaches geology at Sonoma State University. She's a California registered geologist, and she's the author of six whodunits, all of them featuring Emily Hansen, the geologist-turned detective. She also belongs to a murder-mystery writers' group.

"I learn from the other members of the group, including the least experienced writers," she says. " Listening to them talk about writing, helps me not to make the same mistakes I've made again and again."

Andrews has a helpful list of suggestions about the whodunit genre and she spells them out. "Beginning writers often try to explain everything in the first chapter and that's a big mistake," she says. "Readers want to be intrigued. They want the action to start fast so you've got to give them a hook, and take them on a hero's journey. Moreover, the story itself has to have a clear beginning, a clear middle and a resounding conclusion."

The characters are perhaps the chief attraction in Andrews's novels so it's not surprising that she emphasizes the importance of developing the hero, the villain and the supporting cast of good guys, bad guys, cops and criminals.

"People today are reading for the characters," she says. "The sleuth these days, unlike the sleuth of old, must change, learn and impart lessons. That means a character takes risks and becomes wiser. There also has to be a strong antagonist – either the murderer or the victim of murder. In the murder mystery, the tragic figure is usually the killer because that person falls from grace."

While many mystery writers outline their novels before they begin to write, Andrews prefers to find her way as she goes along. There may be false leads and dead ends, but almost always there's a big payoff – either a discovery about her characters or about herself.

"Sometimes I don't know who has committed the murder when I start out," she says. "And sometimes I change my mind about the killer in the middle of the book. I like the challenge of getting deep into the story and then seeing if I can get out of it."

For all her explorations and discoveries, Andrews is respectful of traditional rules and regulations of the genre, and she insists that novices respect the genre itself. "Beginning writers need to recognize the form itself and abide by it," she says. "For me, writing a murder mystery is like writing a sonnet."

Once you've written a murder mystery, Andrews has suggestions about publication. "The first thing is to decide whether you're interested in writing one novel, or if you want to make a lifetime career of it and write a whole series of detective stories," she says. "If it's just one book, I'd suggest that you self-publish. If you want to write a series, then you need to join the professional societies, talk to the pros and learn the business inside and out. I'd suggest, too, that if it's money you're after, don't write murder mysteries. Sell Volvos or work as a geologist for an oil company. That's much more lucrative."

Why does Andrews write whodunits if not for the money?

"I do it for the learning, the personal growth," she says. "In *An Eye for Gold*, I wanted to see if I could reconcile conflicting points of view, not only about gold mining but also about big issues like individual liberty and social responsibility. In the process of writing the novel, I became more aware of what I was consuming and where it comes from. I eat less now than before, and I appreciate food more than ever before. Writing *An Eye for Gold*, made me more respectful of the environment."

Bill Moody

Looking for Chet Baker

I have long enjoyed jazz – bebop, swing, Dixieland and more – all over the States, but I've never really ached for jazz as much as when I've been abroad. I suppose that's because I inevitably grow homesick in Paris, London and Amsterdam, and nothing – except a return ticket – cures that longing for home like the sound of authentic American jazz. Oddly enough, many of the geniuses of jazz have often found themselves revered in Europe far more than on native soil. Like many of our best writers, they've often become expatriates.

Chet Baker – the Oklahoma-born trumpet player and singer – had a loyal following in Europe that kept him going back again and again. Near the end of his life – he died in 1988 – he played in Europe more than he played in America. He had more fans in Europe, too. Baker also had a long-time heroin addiction that plagued him even as he played beautiful music, and that dark side of his life added to his legend.

Baker is, of course, at the heart of Bill Moody's mystery *Looking for Chet Baker*. So is Evan Horne, a piano player who doubles as a detective, and who has appeared in four previous novels by Moody, including *Death of a Tenor Man* and *Bird Lives!* Horne is an admirable sleuth and a soulful musician, and it's easy to understand why Moody has kept him alive in book after book. He has never been so cool or so hot either as he is in *Looking for Chet Baker* and Moody hits all the right notes, too. Granted, the twists and the turns of the plot don't always add up. Mystery writers – even the very best of them – rarely construct airtight narratives, and fans usually find it in themselves to forgive them. Moody's flaws are forgivable because his characters are unforgettable.

It won't spoil the fun, I don't think, if I say that *Looking for Chet Baker* ends dramatically in Monte Rio on the Russian River. There's a colorful description of the Pink Elephant, the town's landmark bar, and a brief passage about some of its colorful patrons, too.

Mostly the book is set in Amsterdam, where American jazz has long had aficionados, and where Baker died at the age of 58, leaving behind a huge body of recorded music. Moody makes the most of Amsterdam and its eccentric Dutch citizens. The city itself comes alive in these pages – the jazz joints, the canals, the familiar tourist attractions and the dark nooks and crannies, too. Little by little, Horne delves deeper and deeper into the city and into the brilliant career and the tragic death of Baker himself.

Did he jump from the window of his hotel? Or was he pushed? There are lots of questions all along the way, and plenty of suspense, too. Now and then, there are humorous moments, especially when Charles ("Ace") Buffington, a buffoonish Professor of English at the University of Nevada at Las Vegas, is on the scene.

When he isn't playing his piano, Evan Horne follows a trail of intriguing clues. He talks to the taciturn Dutch police, explores the notorious red-light district and encounters desperate drug dealers. He also discovers that Humboldt County homegrown is available in the city's marijuana clubs, and that it's "killer weed" indeed.

What *Looking for Chet Baker* has going for it, in addition to the Amsterdam setting, is the music that's either in the background or at the center of the story. Horne describes the jazz he plays with a young expatriate named Fletcher Paige, and you can practically hear it. "I start a vamp, in tempo, just beyond ballad speed," Horne explains. "Fletcher slips in like he's parting a curtain and just suddenly there, sliding into the melody, singing with his horn, catching everybody off guard with his long, elegant lines, at times like cues, floating and lingering like billowy clouds in the air even after they're gone."

There's real poetry here, and the tempo of the story keeps the reader attuned to Bill Moody's moody tale. There's also a lot to be learned about Baker's style of music, and about his deadly addiction. A film crew is in Amsterdam making a documentary about Baker, and Moody follows them around the city.

Looking for Chet Baker is a kind of torch song to one of the 20th century's most moving horn players and jazz singers. If you're inclined to listen to his music, as I was, after reading this mystery about him, Moody provides a handy, selected discography at the back of the book. My favorite Chet Baker CD is *You Can't Go Home Again*. My favorite Baker tune is "My Funny Valentine," which he probably played hundreds of times. There's something innocent and vulnerable about Baker's voice – some-

thing almost boyish. Moody writes with a sense of sweetness and vulner-
ability, too, and that makes his mystery a pleasure to read.

Bill Moody: Solo at the Pink Elephant

One day there will be a plaque in Monte Rio and the people here
will point to it with a sense of pride. The plaque will honor Bill Moody
and it will describe him as a novelist, musician and teacher. It will say that
Moody lived in Monte Rio from 1997 to 2002 and that he wrote his mystery *Looking for Chet Baker* here. Bill Moody will become a local hero.
But this foggy morning no one in Monte Rio seems to know who Bill
Moody is, certainly not the regulars at the Pink Elephant – the bar that
serves as the unofficial town hall and meeting place. Moody sits at a table
in the corner nursing a coke and munching on the popcorn that the bar-
tender – a young woman – has provided free of charge.

Of course, Moody doesn't expect applause and autograph seekers.
After all, he's been a drummer for most of his life. He's been the musician
at the back of the stage. And, as a jazz disc jockey on the radio for much
of his life, he's maintained a low profile, too – a man who's heard but not
often seen. Granted, as a high school and as a college teacher, he's been
front and center, but Bill Moody is the kind of teacher who doesn't hunger
for the spotlight.

Born in Webb City, Missouri in 1941, he moved to southern California with his mother and his father when he was five years old. Both his
parents sang in the church choir, and Bill's mother played the piano and
encouraged him to pursue music. "My friends were into Elvis Presley and
Ricky Nelson," he says. "I didn't get into that. I was listening to Ella
Fitzgerald, Sarah Vaughn and Bobby Hackett." Even as a teenager he
knew he wanted to grow up and become a drummer. All through his
teenage years, he played the drums in the living room.

After graduating from high school in Santa Monica, he did four
years in the Air Force, mostly in Japan, where he discovered the music of
Art Blakey and the Jazz Messengers, Miles Davis and Horace Silver.
Moody played drums in all-black bands and often at all-black clubs. "It
never occurred to me to think twice about that," he says. "I was hired to
play and I played. No one in any of the bands I played with ever mentioned

the color of my skin, and no one in the audience ever did either."

In the mid-1960s, Moody studied at the Berkeley College of Music in Boston. Then, he went on tour with Junior Mance and Jimmy Rushing and traveled from Hermosa Beach to San Francisco, Seattle to Detroit. After that, it was off to Europe where he played in Prague, Hamburg, and London. "I was on the road a lot," Moody says. "It gets old after a while. You go from hotel to concert to hotel to concert to airport." For a while it seemed like he might become another American jazz expatriate, but he returned to the States, attended the University of Nevada at Las Vegas, received an M.A. and taught creative writing.

"There's a big correlation between jazz and writing," Moody says. "A jazz musician will play a standard tune like 'Bye-Bye Blackbird,' and then he'll improvise on the chords. When I write I have a framework. I have a beginning, a middle and an end, but I don't know how I'm going to get there until I do. Like jazz, writing is a process of discovery."

To write *Looking for Chet Baker*, Moody flew to Amsterdam in December of 2000. "I went to the hotel where Chet died," he says. "I wandered around the old quarter and went to some of the jazz clubs. I also learned a lot about Chet right here in Monte Rio. I met a jazz singer named Marigold Hill who lives around the corner and who was a good friend of Chet's. You know he spent time on the Russian River, played in the bars around here and in the annual Jazz Festival."

Moody teaches creative writing at Sonoma State University. He also plays drums all over the Bay Area – from the Volano Deli in Crockett, to the Cobalt Tavern in North Beach. Until recently he played at Pairs Restaurant in Napa. And he's working on a new novel, too, about an American musician living in Czechoslovakia in 1968 just as the Russians invade. It's shaping up as a thriller, not as a murder mystery.

Europe still fascinates Moody, and part of him wouldn't mind going back. "It's ironic," he says. "Jazz is an American art form, but it's appreciated in Europe far more than it is here. Europeans are incredible jazz fans. I wasn't a famous musician but I was always treated like an artist. Chet Baker was treated like a king."

Bill Pronzini

A Wasteland of Strangers

Bill Pronzini's suspenseful crime novel, *A Wasteland of Strangers* is delightfully down home and devilishly intriguing. It has the feel of Mark Twain, Thornton Wilder and David Lynch all wrapped up in one, which is to say that it's folksy and weird and funny.

The main strength of the book is the cast of complex characters, each of whom tells the gripping story of his or her own turbulent life, and each of whom advances the story of a mysterious stranger named John Faith, who arrives in a wasteland of a town named Pomo, where everyone is more or less a stranger to everyone else, though everyone seems to be as friendly as all getout.

"Pomo's a deceptive place. Looks nice and peaceful, but underneath it's a snake pit," John Faith tells Audrey Sixkiller soon after she's narrowly escaped rape at the hands of an unidentified assailant, and shortly after he's been named as the prime suspect in a sensational case involving the brutal murder of a beautiful, over-sexed widow named Storm Casey who has almost every man in town knocking on her bedroom door.

It's no wonder that John Faith is public enemy number one in Pomo County and at the top of almost everyone's most wanted list. After all Faith is the outsider, the loner, the drifter. After all he's big and he's ugly. Indeed, John Faith looks guilty, looks guilty as sin, and looks, too, like he's ready-made to play the part of the fall guy in Storm Casey's murder.

Richard Novak, the emotionally-distressed Chief of Police, is out to get him, and so is Douglas Kent, the alcoholic editor of the *Pomo Advocate*, the only newspaper in town.

But John Faith also has his friends, especially a pregnant teenage girl named Tricia Marx; a waitress named Lori Banner, who has been battered by her jealous husband Earle; and, of course, Audrey Sixkiller, a local Pomo Indian who has graduated from UC Berkeley and who has come home hoping to bring the spirit of her ancestors into the sad lives of her neighbors.

A Wasteland of Strangers also tells the tale of George Petrie, the remorseful banker who steals from his own bank, and the tale, too, of the Muñoz brothers, one of whom is good, and one of whom is evil, one who loves and one who hates.

Bill Pronzini gets inside the skin of all his characters. He knows what they drink, and where they work, and how they walk, and what they're thinking, and how they talk. Reading this book is like listening to the voices of the people on Main Street in a small town, a town that could be anywhere in America, a town that offers a parable for our time.

The novel has something for almost everyone: action and adventure; love and sex; danger, deception; and an ending in which the crimes are solved, the innocent are rewarded and the guilty are punished.

If you've been to the movies and you haven't found that big, thrilling picture you've been waiting for, then *A Wasteland of Strangers* just might be for you. It isn't on the big screen, of course, but it has the best of big-screen chills and thrills, of heroes and heroines you can't help but love, and villains you love to hate.

Bill Pronzini: Petaluma's Prolific Author

Somewhere in Bill Pronzini's life there's a mystery, though what it is he won't say, at least not today, and maybe not ever. Bill Pronzini is that kind of guy – a guy who doesn't go around town talking about private matters.

"My life has been chaotic at times, but I don't want to get into it," he says during a pleasant mid-morning telephone conversation from Petaluma, where his Italian ancestors settled around the turn of the century, and where he was born in 1943 and went to high school, and where he lives with his wife Marcia Muller who also writes fiction.

"You can't control situations in real life, but you can control them in fiction," Pronzini says. "When you're writing mysteries you can eliminate most of the chaos and make almost everything come out right. You can punish the bad guys and make most of the good guys triumph. I suppose that's why mysteries appeal to me. And, of course, I'm also interested in why people commit crimes."

If the citizens of Petaluma have been rightfully celebrated over the

years for raising chickens, then Bill Pronzini, Petaluma's most prolific
author, ought to be celebrated for raising novels. He's certainly raised
enough of them – nearly fifty at last count – and he's certainly won enough
prizes – two Shamus Awards and nominations five times over for the
Edgar Allen Poe Award.

Pronzini grew up reading kid mysteries and then the adult variety.
He wrote his first novel at 12, and though he's had odd jobs from time to
time – parking cars and selling plumbing supplies – he's never stopped
writing for long, or run out of ideas, or the sheer energy it takes to turn out
novel after novel after novel.

His first published novel, *The Stalker*, which is set, in part, along
the Petaluma River, appeared in 1971. Over the next two decades
Petaluma figured in several of his books, including *Quicksilver* and *With
an Extreme Burning*.

A Wasteland of Strangers takes place in a colorful, crime-infested
northern California county called Pomo. The county's main town is Pomo,
the major newspaper is the *Pomo Advocate*, and Pomo High is where
Audrey Sixkiller, a Pomo Indian and the novel's heroine, teaches California history.

"Pomo is based loosely on Lake County," Pronzini says. "But it's
not reflective of Lake County. I started work on the book about two years
ago. I went up there and did research on the history of Lake County, on the
Pomo Indians, and on small-town newspapers, too."

A Wasteland of Strangers, like Pronzini's other novels, is a novel
of ideas, as the title suggests. "I've been doing a lot of fiction about alienation in modern society, and I wanted to do another one along those lines,"
he said. "I also wanted to do a book about misconceptions based on appearances. We make too many spur-of-the-moment decisions about people
based on what they look like."

Pronzini says he doesn't burn out writing crime and detective
fiction because he has "an active imagination," and because he treats
writing "as a job, a business." It also seems to help that he often collabo-
rates with his wife Marcia. "We have the same approach," he says. "We
exchange our work. We act as sounding boards. We function as each
other's editor."

Marcia Muller

Dead Midnight

Sharon McCone – Marcia Muller's San Francisco sleuth – isn't as spry as she was when she appeared in her very first novel, *Edwin of the Iron Shoes,* nearly 20 years ago. Now she's middle-aged and in the midst of a mid-life crisis. "Over the years I'd seen too much violence, too many evil deeds done as the result of greed, cowardice, or just plain stupidity," McCone explains in *Dead Midnight*, the 21st novel in which she doggedly gathers clues and solves all sorts of intriguing mysteries. "I was on over-load," she continues, "and wanted nothing more than to stow the memories in my mental bank vault, go home, and indulge in those mundane, com-forting rituals allowed to other people."

Twenty-one novels can take a toll on a detective, even one as crafty as McCone. It can also take a toll on a writer, even one as creative as Muller, diva of women's detective fiction. If you set your novels in the Bay Area again and again, as Muller has done, you eventually run out of new neighborhoods, new landmarks and new kinds of characters to de-scribe. Sometimes Muller goes over familiar territory. And sometimes she seems to be on overload, like her own detective. But she's a professional, and so is Sharon McCone. No matter what, they both get the job done. In the end the case is closed, the book is finished.

In *Dead Midnight*, McCone breaks new ground by investigating the suicide of a Japanese-American writer named Roger Nagasawa who works for a hip online magazine called *Insite*. (Nagasawa jumps from the Richmond-San Rafael Bridge, or was he pushed over the edge?) It's a complicated case of suicide, murder and missing persons that's made all the more complicated by the fact that McCone's brother, Joey, who has been popping pills and abusing alcohol in sordid surroundings, takes his own life. As usual, McCone explores a whole world. In this case it's the cool, calculating world of dot-comers and venture capitalists, a perfect setting for a murder or two, and Muller does a good job of capturing the nuisances of Bay Area corporate culture circa 2000. Technology is in the saddle and privacy has been all but eliminated at the work place.

Then, too, as usual, McCone is all over the map of San Francisco in her vintage MG, firing questions at all times of day and night – even "dead midnight" – at eccentric San Francisco characters. There's the colorful landlady Jane Harris, and there's the intrepid reporter J.D. Smith, both of whom add an element of spicy San Francisco history and culture. Of Jane Harris, McCone explains, "She'd been married to a minor Beat poet in the fifties, a minor rock musician in the sixties, a minor artist in the seventies, and in the eighties a major distributor of soft drinks." That's the kind of insight that makes this book delightful.

Muller has a wry sense of humor that lights up *Dead Midnight.* She writes cleanly, crisply, sometimes poetically and now and then she relaxes her grip on the plot long enough to let her private eye break down and pour out her innermost feelings. After all, McCone is a female private eye. Unlike her tough guy colleagues with their fedoras and trench coats, she's supposed to be emotional. Moreover, it wouldn't feel right if she didn't have house cats and her trustworthy woman's intuition to tell her what to do when all else is lost. Of course, she also has a .357 Magnum – which she keeps locked up in a vault most of the time – and she knows how to use a gun as well as Sam Spade or Travis McGee. Of course, as always it's McCone herself who is at the emotional center of this book, and it's her character and personality, as well as her observations about people and the city of San Francisco, that give the novel its pizzazz.

Still, somewhere near the end, *Dead Midnight* feels as though it's going to break down under its own weight. There's just too much information and perhaps too many suspects. Fewer characters and fewer subplots might help to lighten the load. When McCone finally wraps up the case – with the help of her cell phone and a computer – and takes off in her own airplane for a vacation in Mendocino County, you're ready to take off with her. You hope she gets a much-needed rest before she's back in business, exploring the Bay Area once again and making her life the kind of open book that lures you back for more murder and more mystery.

Marcia Muller: Speaking from Los Alegres (or is it Petaluma?)

The following interview took place on October 11, 2002, soon after

Marcia Muller returned home to Petaluma from a vacation in Oregon.

Jonah: Is there a mother of the modern woman's detective story?
Marcia: In the late 1970s there were a lot of women writing detective fiction. I happened to find a publisher sooner than the others. At this point I think I'm in line to be the grandmother of them all.
Jonah: Was there a decisive turning point for women's detective fiction?
Marcia: It was 1982. Sue Grafton was published for the first time that year and so was Sara Paretsky. My first novel had been published in 1977, but I couldn't get my second book into print until 1982.
Jonah: Sounds like there might be a connection to the women's liberation movement of the 1970s.
Marcia: The novels were definitely a byproduct. In the real world there were women working as cops, lawyers and detectives. Women began to write about them, and publishers came to realize that it wasn't as far-fetched an idea as it once seemed to have fictional detectives.
Jonah: You've said that you like Ross MacDonald better than Dashiell Hammett.
Marcia: I like Raymond Chandler, too. He and MacDonald appeal to me more than Hammett.
Jonah: Why is that?
Marcia: There's something about the way they look at and describe California. I'm not a native, but when I came here I fell in love with the state. When you read MacDonald and Chandler you can tell what California was like when they were writing. I try to do the same thing in my books.
Jonah: Are detective novels realistic?
Marcia: They are and they aren't. Usually the crimes themselves are preposterous. The reader has to suspend disbelief. But I try to make the situation and the characters as true to life as possible. Real detective cases are often boring. There's a lot of tracing of husbands for child support. The computer has narrowed the dramatic possibilities.
Jonah: You've written a lot of novels, and I imagine that you repeat yourself.
Marcia: It happens all the time and so I go back and edit. The worst is that I forgot to put things in, like someone's appearance.
Jonah: The basics?
Marcia: Yes, like what a character is wearing and how they look. At book

signings readers will ask me in such and such a book what did you mean?
Usually I can't remember the plot of a book I wrote 10 or 15 years ago, let
alone the meaning.

Jonah: When you look back at McCone's long career, what highpoints do
you see?

Marcia: In the beginning, Sharon was a cheerleader. Over the years she
became less bright-eyed. It isn't that she was naïve. It's hard to describe it.
Sharon was a cheerleader in high school and she went on being a kind of
cheerleader in life. With *Wolf in the Shadows* the series became much
darker, and with *Listen to the Silence,* Sharon learned that she was
adopted. That made for a big difference in her personality.

Jonah: How many books ahead can you see?

Marcia: I'm usually two books out. I just delivered my next book, *Cyanide
Wells,* which will be published in July and I have the basic outline for the
McCone after that one. I'm also working on two "stand-alones" as they're
called – novels that aren't part of the McCone series.

Jonah: Your husband Bill Pronzini also writes detective fiction.

Marcia: We borrow from one another all the time. We both set books in
the fictional town of Los Alegres, which readers complain they can't find
on a map of Sonoma County, but Los Alegres is Petaluma, of course. I
love creating fictional towns. I've also created a county called Soledad
that's between Humboldt and Mendocino. You won't find it on any map,
either, though I've made my own map of the place.

Jonah: What else are you working on now?

Marcia: *Time of the Wolves*, a collection of short stories I have written
about the American West. It will be published next summer along with
Cyanide Wells.

Jonah: What defines "the West" for you?

Marcia: A certain pioneer spirit, the urge to move, to go and to see more.
A lot of the stories in *Time of the Wolves* have a crime theme. I can't seem
to get away from crime and its repercussions.

Part IV:
Voyagers,
Visionaries,
Historians

George Rathmell

Realms of Gold:
The Colorful Writers of San Francisco, 1850-1950

Until I was 30, I lived most of my life in and around New York. Like a great many New Yorkers, I thought of California as a mythological place. Of course, I wasn't the first to mythologize the Golden State. California has long been a place of mythical proportions – "El Norte" to immigrants from the south, "Continent's End" to pioneers from the east, "Turtle Island" to the Indians. Long before I arrived here, I created my own myth of California, cobbled together from novels like John Steinbeck's *The Grapes of Wrath* and Nathaniel West's *The Day of the Locust,* and from movies like Howard Hawks's *The Big Sleep* and Roman Polanski's *Chinatown.*

My California was dark and dangerous – an American nightmare where the police were corrupt, millionaires were criminals, and men in power betrayed their own families and friends time and again. Not surprisingly, I identified with Tom Joad, Steinbeck's fugitive Okie, and with Jake Gittes, Polanksi's detective who is doomed to failure.

Of course, I had to see the state for myself, and when I finally arrived in 1975, I was surprised. California struck me as elusive and mysterious, a mirage that rose out of the Pacific – a vast nation within a nation itself.

What continues to amaze me is how much California is still mythologized. Not long ago I met a French professor who looked at me with pity and who said how sorry he was that I lived in California – a land without culture. "Of course, you can't have culture in the sun," he said.

Still, the myths of California are dying slowly, even among die-hard New Yorkers. In a 1998 issue of *The New Yorker* that was devoted to California, an article entitled "Alta California" proclaimed "San Francisco is particularly receptive to poets, novelists and journalists." New York literati may take this as late-breaking news, but it will certainly not be news to most of the readers who live and work in Alta California.

It certainly isn't news to George Rathmell, the author of *Realms of*

Gold: The Colorful Writers of San Francisco, 1850-1950. Rathmell graduated from UC Berkeley in the mid-1950s. He has been a lifelong student and scholar of the literature of Alta California. Nowadays he lives and writes in Sea Ranch, right on the edge of the Pacific Ocean.

At the start of *Realms of Gold*, Rathmell explains that like Paris, San Francisco has its own "cachet" – its own unique charm. The city by the Bay is "restless and improbable," he writes, and though he never quite captures that "cachet" – perhaps it's too elusive, too mercurial to be captured in words – he does sketch its seductive charms.

There are so many good writers in this book – Bret Harte, Mark Twain, Ambrose Bierce, Robinson Jeffers, Dashiell Hammett, John Steinbeck and Kenneth Rexroth – and Rathmell selects quotations from their work to suggest the "cachet" of San Francisco. "San Francisco is a mad city – inhabited for the most part by perfectly insane people," Rudyard Kipling wrote. Frank Norris noted that "things can happen in San Francisco…There is an indefinable air." And Steinbeck observed, "I felt I owned the city as much as it owned me."

Reading this book is a lot like watching scenes from bohemian life. We see the San Francisco writers in restaurants, bookstores and clubs, most notably the Bohemian Club, which was founded in 1872, and which was at the heart of the city's cultural life for decades. Rathmell's descriptions are so vivid that you can almost smell the pungent smoke of cigars, almost hear the roar of the crowd along Market Street. You listen to conversations about literature and the arts. You meet the wives and the lovers of the writers, and you're caught up in their passions, their romantic affairs, their triumphs and tragedies.

What's more, the individual stories are set against an epic canvas of historical events – the Gold Rush, the Civil War, the earthquake of 1906, the stock market crash of 1929, and World War II, which transformed California forever.

Realms of Gold is rich ore, indeed, though it doesn't have everything I'd have liked. Rathmell is strong on literary history, but sometimes he's thin when it comes to literary criticism and commentary. Then too he covers so many writers that notable figures like Ambrose Bierce and Kenneth Rexroth, among others, don't receive the attention they deserve.

What I did especially like was discovering little-known writers: Mary Austin, whose *The Land of Rain* is a classic of literature about the desert; and Yone Noguchi, the romantic Japanese poet and author of *Seen and Unseen; or, Monologues of a Homeless Snail*, which appeared in 1896, but which still seems alive and fresh. Rathmell might have included other writers including Toshio Mori, the novelist and short story writer. Mori was born in Oakland in 1910, and though he was published in the 1930s, much of his work didn't appear until the 1970s and 1980s, a time that falls outside Rathmell's boundaries.

Realms of Gold is an excellent introduction to the poets, novelists and journalists who lived in and wrote about Alta California. It reveals the richness of our literary history, and our cultural diversity, too.

George Rathmell: Writers Are Hiding in the Redwoods

George Rathmell lives in Gualala, a small town on the north coast of northern California. It's a long way from the centers of literary influence and power – there isn't a single bookstore in the town. But there are excellent, often invisible writers all around him, including J. California Cooper, the award-winning African-American author of *A Piece of Mine*, *Homemade Love*, and *The Future Has a Past*. "Novelists, poets and short story writers are hiding in the redwoods," he says. "Many of them, like J. California Cooper, are very private. They aren't looking for publicity or attention. They'd rather be left alone to write."

Born in Berkeley in 1931, Rathmell attended San Francisco State and UC Berkeley in the era of the Beats. "I didn't know any of the Beat writers," he says. "I was an observer. In North Beach I'd hang out at Vesuvios, where the Beats gathered, and at the Hungry i, I heard comedians and satirists like Mort Sahl. It was very edgy stuff."

California literature was rarely taught in schools or in colleges when Rathmell was a student, but he developed an avid interest in the literature of the Golden State from an early age. One of his high school teachers, John Ryan, had been a friend of Jack London's, and Ryan exerted a strong influence. "He planted the seeds in my imagination," he says. "Later on I became fascinated with Robert Louis Stevenson, and from then I read voraciously in California literature. What fascinated me about the writers of the 19th century was that they knew one another and were influenced by each other's work. That closeness doesn't seem to exist anymore."

Rathmell has thought a great deal about California writers and their work. When I asked him why some California writers remain local or regional, and why others become nationally and even internationally known, he said that the crucial factor was talent. "Take Bret Harte and Mark Twain," he said. "Harte's talent is limited. Twain's is immense and so he's read and enjoyed much more widely."

If he had to write volume two of his book *Realms of Gold,* he isn't sure which authors he'd include. And he's not sure which of today's writers will go one being read 50 or 100 years from now. "Danielle Steele is certainly the most popular contemporary California writer, but I don't think she's very good," he said. "And I don't know what the future has in store for Isabel Allende's books. She might be all but forgotten in years to come."

He does feel as strongly today about John Steinbeck's *Grapes of Wrath* as he did when he first read it. "It's not dated at all," he says. "We don't have refugees from the Dust Bowl, but we certainly do have Mexican migrants, and their plight is immense."

Rathmell thinks that much of American popular culture starts out in California and moves east. But when it comes to the written word he feels that New York sets trends. "The main publishers are all there, and so are the influential magazines," he says. "Still, California literature is a very rich field, and I'm glad to see that students today are exposed to the literary legends of their own tribe. And I'm delighted that magazines like *The New Yorker* are acknowledging the literary creativity of Alta California."

Tolbert McCarroll

Thinking with the Heart

In the 1950s, only three religious groups were widely recognized in America: Protestants, Catholics and Jews, almost always listed in that order. Mostly, they talked to themselves; "interfaith groups" – as they were called – were few and far between. In public schools, the day started with the Lord's Prayer, and yet prayer, along with sex and politics, was a topic that students and teachers rarely discussed.

Then, the spiritually hungry 1960s erupted. The old walls that separated religious groups came tumbling down, figuratively if not literally, and Americans en masse pursued bearded and baby-faced gurus, holy men and self-anointed goddesses from Thailand to Tibet and from India to Indian reservations in God-forsaken places.

Tolbert McCarroll, a lay monk at Starcross Monastery in Mendocino County, was an ardent spiritual seeker in the 1960s. Born to a traditional Catholic family in Mississippi during the Depression, he grew restless with orthodox Catholicism as a young man, and for years he energetically pursued a wide variety of religious experiences. "I bought a meditation pillow and imagined myself a Japanese Zen Buddhist," he writes in *Thinking with the Heart*, perhaps the most heartfelt of his many books about spiritual matters. "At various times I was also pretending to be a Hopi, a Sufi and a Shaker." McCarroll was not alone. The last several decades have witnessed a spiritual mass migration of Americans.

In *Thinking with the Heart,* McCarroll looks back at his own life, and explains that the religions associated with cultures not his own rarely fulfilled his deepest need for spiritual sustenance. His book tells the story, in large part, of how and why he returned to the religion into which he was born. "I am a Catholic because that is my culture," he writes. But McCarroll is also a Catholic with a heart big and strong enough to include the prayers, poems and preachings of Zen monks, Jewish mystics and Protestant ministers.

If we take catholic (with a small c) to mean all-inclusive, then this book is clearly catholic. McCarroll also carves out a specific tradition within Catholicism (with a capital C) that accentuates the mystical and the humanistic rather than the institutional. So, his spiritual ancestors include European Catholics like St. Francis of Assisi, Teresa of Avila and Ignatius Loyola. You'll also find that McCarroll admires Nicholas von Flue, an Alpine farmer who belonged to the 14th century group called the "Friends of God," as well as Dietrich Bonhoeffer, the German Protestant pastor who opposed the Nazis and was executed by them.

A rigorous intellectual foe of intolerance and orthodoxy, McCarroll describes Jesus as *the* original freethinker and non-conformist. "Jesus himself was not a Christian," he writes. "He was an unschooled Jewish layman who ignored established religious traditions and institutions." In McCarroll's view, Jesus was an "oddball" and a "sage" – a kind of Zen holy man who defied the law and order of his own day. In one of the most vivid and compelling sections of the book, the author describes the crucifixion of Jesus Christ. He sees and hears the world as he imagines Jesus saw it and heard it when he was "stripped naked...on the cross of shame." Yes, of course, reread the gospels according to Matthew, Mark, Luke and John, and then please read the story of Christ according to Tolbert McCarroll.

Thinking with the Heart is a visionary work, but it also offers a series of practical stepping stones for people, like most of us, who live in the midst of crisis and chaos. What McCarroll seeks – and what he hopes his readers will also seek – is the "stillpoint of creation." With great simplicity and clarity, he describes the ordinary daily activities – walking, meditating, and bearing witness – that can open the doors to the sacred and provide a sense of inner peace.

There's a refreshing candor in these pages. McCarroll doesn't claim to be a saint, doesn't pretend to be one, either. Like most of us, he stumbles and confesses his flaws – his impatience with other people, for example. Still, a saintly quality shines through this book. I recommend it for any season, no matter what church, temple or synagogue you attend. And if you're an agnostic or a pagan, the chances are you'll also find McCarroll's book spiritually uplifting.

Brother Toby: Mendocino Monk with a Message of Hope

It's December and Tolbert McCarroll – Brother Toby to all the world – has Christmas on his mind. As usual, he and the sisters at Starcross Monastery in Mendocino County are making Christmas wreaths from silvertip fir trees that grow near Mt. Shasta. "We shipped 2,600 today," he says. "Only 4,000 or so to go. Of course, we have a lot of volunteers, including Gaye and John LeBaron – the whole LeBaron family, in fact. All the money that we earn goes to Starcross. It's our main source of financial support."

With his white beard and wooden crucifix, Brother Toby looks very much like a monk. But he's a jovial monk – a monk who rejoices in life. His cap is bright orange, his sweater emerald green. He's been celebrating Christmas for as long as he can remember. Almost all of his Christmases have been memorable, but one in particular – December 25, 1941, just weeks after Pearl Harbor – stands out more than any other. "It was the most intense Christmas in my life," he says. "I was ten years old. It was wartime. All of a sudden, young men from my high school began to disappear. All around me there was an awareness of death and loss. But people were especially close to one another. They were very loving. The war encouraged sharing and generosity."

At the age of 12, Tolbert McCarroll decided he wanted to become a priest. His parents, who were devout Catholics, sent him to Mount Angel Abbey, which was run by the Benedictine Monks in Oregon. He remained there for three years, then changed his mind and finished his senior year at a public high school. "I mostly didn't have a positive experience at Mount Angel," he says. "In those days the Catholic Church tended to be dogmatic; the Catholic way was supposed to be the only way to find God. You couldn't even use music by non-Catholic composers in church. On the positive side, I developed a respect for the contemplative side of Catholicism."

As a young man, McCarroll became an agnostic and an existentialist. He read Camus, worked as an attorney and joined the National Lawyers Guild. He also married and raised a family. In the 1960s, he began to rediscover his own Catholic heritage, and then nearly thirty years ago he helped to create Starcross. "At first it was hard," he says. "Our house of worship was a teepee. Then, it was an old barn with bats that was freezing in winter. Now, we have a lovely little chapel. I'm content with the life I lead here. I experience no want. This morning I came out of the chapel and the sun was breaking through the fog. Everything sparkled. It was beautiful."

Thinking with the Heart is his eighth book. The first five books were about spiritual matters. The last two were memoirs that describe his work with children afflicted with AIDS. "When I wrote *Thinking with the Heart,* I was thinking of my own children," he says. "I meant this book to be my spiritual will and testament to them. Finding the right voice was hard. I didn't want to be preachy or whiney. I wanted a voice that would resonate ten years from now, and I wanted to be hopeful."

So far, critical reactions to the book have been mixed. One reviewer objected to McCarroll's pluralistic approach and his pantheism. "I plead guilty to pantheism," he says. "I do find God in nature. I know that people find God in many different ways. It would be arrogant to say that there is only one way. I also plead guilty to the pluralistic approach."

The annual Christmas celebrations at Starcross will be simpler than they have been, and that's agreeable to Brother Toby. "September 11 has sharpened our perceptions," he says. "The kids who live here with us have asked that we cut back on the materialistic side of Christmas. We'll try to be more aware of our place in the world, and we'll try not to take anything for granted. At night we'll go on star walks, and in the morning we'll rise early and greet the dawn. This Christmas will be a time of healing. Like December 7, 1941, 9/11 shows us that we need to make peace in our own personal lives."

Ray Raphael

The First American Revolution: Before Lexington and Concord

This Fourth of July there will be beer, barbecue and baseball, of course. As always, I'll wave my American flag at the parade, and spend a quiet afternoon with friends. I expect that there will be patriotic speeches and commentaries from media pundits about what it means to be an American and about America's place in the world. And yet, in the wake of 9/11, there's no way the Fourth of July could be the same that it has been in recent memory. Patriotism has taken on new meaning.

Ray Raphael's *The First American Revolution* contributes to the on-going national debate about American freedom and American security, America's past and America's future. In its own quiet way, this carefully researched book about a lost chapter in our history invites readers to think about why we celebrate the Fourth of July – and why we ought to celebrate it. *The First American Revolution* suggests that ordinary, unsung Americans embody the best of American values, and that at its best America is a country of grass roots democracy. Moreover, the author insists that revolutions need not be violent, and that ordinary Americans don't need leaders to tell them when or why to rebel. In short, this is revisionist history with profound reverberations for the present day.

The First American Revolution isn't about the revolution that dominates most textbooks about American history. There is almost nothing here about the Declaration of Independence, Thomas Jefferson, John Adams and the founding brothers, as they've come to be called. Raphael's book is about the peaceful rebellion that took place in 1774 in rural Massachusetts – not in Boston or in any other big city – to protest British rule.

When Governor Thomas Gage outlawed town meetings and abolished local elections, farmers and artisans took to the streets to topple his appointed officials. Oddly enough the protestors were extraordinarily well behaved. There was no indiscriminate mob action, and there were no military battles. No hostages were taken and no ultimatums were delivered. There were no charismatic leaders, either, no powerful organizations, and no resounding manifestoes or pamphlets. Despite the paucity of dramatic material, the author has managed to convey a sense of heightened historical drama.

As Raphael tells it, the people of Massachusetts simply rose up en masse and unseated the British authorities in Worcester, Salem, Great Barrington and elsewhere – and then began to create a genuinely democratic society all on their own. They were not impoverished, and they were not brutally oppressed, Raphael explains. "People do not have to be reduced to great depths of poverty before they rebel," he writes. It's a heroic story and it's all the more compelling because it has been largely ignored.

When historians of the American Revolution write about the key political events of 1774, they usually focus on the First Congressional Congress that met in Philadelphia and that attracted prominent citizens like Samuel Adams. *The First American Revolution* looks at power and protest in the hinterlands. It looks at the people, not at famous historical figures. And it argues that our own radical past has been kept from us. Our ancestors were far more revolutionary than the history books and the politicians would have us believe, Raphael insists. They really did want social and political equality. Moreover, the author argues that the American Revolution that began in 1776 wasn't as glorious as it has often been made out to be. The war with the British wreaked havoc on the economy, and at the end of the war, society was less democratic than it was at the start. Ideals were lost and betrayed; the rich were richer, the poor were poorer.

The First American Revolution makes ample use of 18th century documents – private letters and journals as well as town records. Reading them you get the feel for the language, the ideas and the values of colonial Massachusetts. The correspondence between Governor Thomas Gage and Lord Dartmouth – the British secretary of state for the colonies – is especially vivid. So, for example, Dartmouth found it hard to believe that Gage was defeated by "a tumultuous Rabble, without any Appearance of general Concert, or without any Head to advise, or Leader to conduct."

The strength of this book is that it focuses on the rebellion in the small towns of western Massachusetts. In doing so, however, it neglects the larger, bigger picture of insurrection across the Atlantic seaboard. Even a glimpse or two of what was happening elsewhere – in Philadelphia and in Boston for example – in 1774 would provide a fuller picture. Raphael says that, "The rebellion in rural Massachusetts led directly to the establishment of home rule throughout the colonies," but he doesn't explain how or why that happened.

Moreover, he feels that the rebellion of 1774 "set a standard for direct political participation that has not been bettered since." Perhaps it has not been bettered. But what about the reconstruction governments in the South after the Civil War, when African-Americans took part in political life for the first time and brought about profound social and economic changes? And what about the civil rights movement of the 1960s when ordinary people took history into their own hands, broke the back of legal segregation and won the right to vote? Participatory democracy has defined much of the American political tradition.

Perhaps *The First American Revolution* might best be read in conjunction with Raphael's own *A People's History of the American Revolution* which describes the bigger historical picture. For those who enjoy a tale of history off the well-beaten path, *The First American Revolution* ought to be pleasing. For populists, it should be inspiring.

Ray Raphael: The People's Historian

Ray Raphael lives in remote Humboldt County, but he's spent a lot of time over the past few years in Worcester, Massachusetts. It's a long way to go for a story, and many of the ordinary people he's met in Massachusetts have been puzzled by his transcontinental journey. "You're a guy from California. What are you doing here?" he's been asked again and again, most recently when he spoke in April to a large audience at the American Antiquarian Society. "I told those incredulous people that I'm a reporter and that I've been following a hot story," Raphael says during a phone conversation from his home in Redway.

The hot story he's been following took place in Worcester in 1774 – more than 200 years ago. It's a story that he's told in *The First American Revolution*, his book about the popular uprising that unseated British imperial power and preserved that cornerstone of New England democracy – the town meeting.

From the time he was a high school student in New York, Raphael has been fascinated by people's history – history from the bottom up, the history of ordinary folk, not leaders. It started when he read B.A. Bodkin's *Lay My Burden Down*, a collection of narratives by former black slaves that was compiled in the 1930s. Raphael's interest in people's history continued in the early 1960s when he worked in the civil rights movement, first in North Carolina, where he helped to register black voters and to desegregate the all-white swimming pool in Raleigh, and later in Mississippi where he volunteered for Freedom Summer, along with hundreds of other Northern college students – like Mario Savio.

"I took part in the making of history," Raphael says. "What I saw on the ground and in the media were two totally different things. On TV they'd show Martin Luther King, Jr. making a speech. There was little or nothing about the young grassroots activists who put their lives on the line every day."

Raphael moved to Humboldt County in the late 1960s and, there too, he saw how local people made decisions that affected their own lives. He saw democracy in action. Raphael turned his own home into a public school and taught math, science and history – people's history. "We were three-and-a-half hours from the district office," he says. "We could pursue education and learning without rule from above."

His first book, *An Everyday History of Somewhere* is subtitled "Being the true story of Indians, deer, homesteaders, potatoes, loggers, trees, fishermen, salmon, & other living things in the backwoods of northern California." Published in 1974, it's still the best history of Humboldt County. Ever since then, Raphael has been writing everyday histories that historians and biographers have often forgotten or neglected.

"We like to think of our founding fathers as men in fine clothing standing around a table," he says. "We like to think of British soldiers mowing down innocent colonists. The true story is a lot different. In 1774 in rural Massachusetts, the common people took to the streets and stood up to their British rulers. They weren't victims. In fact, they bullied the British."

Raphael doesn't care much for leaders of any kind, including George W. Bush. "Since 9/ 11 we've been told that we ought to rally behind our leaders," he says. "That's antithetical to the spirit of democracy. What's inspiring to me are the ways that ordinary people have responded, as individuals and on their own initiative to that immense tragedy."

Lee Torliatt

Golden Memories of the Redwood Empire

Okay local history buffs, take this test please. Answer true or false.

Question # 1. In 1920, a mob broke into the county jail and lynched three men who had been arrested in Santa Rosa, after the murder of several law enforcement officers.

Question # 2. During World War II, German POWs worked – under armed guard – on Sonoma County farms.

Question # 3. After World War II, professional and semi-professional sports teams – with names like the Bonecrushers and the Leghorns – played before large, enthusiastic crowds.

Sorry, the answers aren't provided in this review. You can find them and lots more information in Lee Torliatt's *Golden Memories of the Redwood Empire*, a colorful account of people and places in Sonoma County from the 1840s to the 1940s. Torliatt's tome isn't definitive. Sometimes, the book is more personal than historical and there are gaps, too. But overall, *Golden Memories* is a gold mine of lore and legend. It ought to delight both local history buffs and newcomers to the area eager to learn about this region's turbulent past. There are ten chapters, beginning with "Moving West" and "The Early Years" and ending with "Demon Rum" and "Sports." Along the way, Torliatt writes about fires, earthquakes and epidemics in a style that's informative, entertaining and humorous. "If anything was sacred in Petaluma, it was the chicken," he writes.

There are fascinating profiles of ordinary folk who did the work of the community day in and day out. There are also profiles of famous personages: M.C. Meeker, the lumber baron; G. W. Dutton, the pioneer farmer; and David Wharf, who reputedly brought the first chickens to the county. The man who might steal the whole show is H.W. (Bert) Kerrigan, the public relations wizard, who created National Egg Day in 1918, and helped make Petaluma into the chicken and egg center of the western world.

Torliatt has culled valuable personal accounts from 19th-century memoirs. I especially like the recollections of Sarepta Turner Ross, who arrived in Sebastopol from Missouri in 1854. "We did not have sawmills to make lumber for building our houses, so the men had to go into the redwoods and hew out the lumber," she wrote. "Jasper O'Farrell owned O'Farrell hill where there was a large body of redwood timber. He sold the trees standing. The farmers bought them, chopped them down and worked them into pickets, rails, and posts to fence the land." Sounds like hard work!

The author has also interviewed dozens of residents about their own lives and the lives of their ancestors. As he makes clear, different individuals sometimes tell very different stories about the same people. "It's not clear whether Peter Torliatt, Sr., a teenager living on the French-Italian border, left home because he wanted to avoid service in the military or because he was accused of throwing a rock at a Catholic priest in the village," he writes. "It depends whether one believes the story told by his daughter Theresa, born in 1890, or his son Peter, Jr., born in 1897."

There's an excellent section about the fate of the Japanese-Americans who lived in Sonoma County and were evacuated at the start of World War II. For example, Jim Miyano, who played high school football in Petaluma, was taken by train from Santa Rosa to Merced and from there to Camp Amache, Colorado where he and thousands of other Japanese-Americans were held captive during the war.

One hundred black-and-white photographs – many of them from the Torliatt family collection – accompany the text. There's one of Jim Miyano feeding chickens. Another shows two young women on the Petaluma River. A third offers a nostalgic view of downtown Santa Rosa in the late 1920s. The photos alone are worth the price of admission.

Lee Torliatt: Man About Town

I've lived and worked in Sonoma County for 26 years and I still feel like an outsider. Maybe I always will. I didn't arrive here until I was in my mid-thirties. By then, I'd already been shaped by the small town where I was born and where I grew up – Huntington, New York – the same town where my father was born and grew up. So, I know what it's like to be a native as well as an outsider.

Lee Torliatt knows both sides, too. Born in Petaluma in 1933, to parents who were born here, he attended St. Vincent's High School – when it cost $10 a year to attend – and then Santa Rosa Junior College. In the late 1940s, he wrote sports for *The Press Democrat* – his column was called "Press Box Splinters." And for decades he taught government and economics to several generations of students at Santa Rosa High School and Piner High School. You might say that Lee Torliatt has been a man about town and that he's been the talk of the town.

"I know a lot of people in Sonoma County," he says. "A lot of people know me. It feels good to have a sense of roots."

We're standing in Torliatt's study in the house in Bennett Valley where he's lived since 1965 – the house where he lived with his wife and daughter. On the walls there are dozens of stunning black-and-white photos of family members and friends. Torliatt points to his father Peter who's wearing a cap and overalls at the auto body shop where he worked. Here's his mother Bernice and his two brothers Don and Ken in a rowboat on the Klamath River during a summer vacation. There's the grandmother who taught school, and here's a group of bearded men in black hats and black coats who look like they've stepped out of a Hollywood western. "I'm the last one in my family who recognizes most of the people in these photos," Torliatt says. "If it goes to the next generation, forget it."

When he started to trace his genealogy, Torliatt knew a lot about his father's side and very little about his mother's side. "Doing the re-search was like being a detective," he says. "One story led to another." Finally, he was back in the 19th century, learning how his mother's ances-tors, the Wards, crossed the American continent – a journey that took two years.

There's a lot of history in Torliatt's own life and times, of course, and it doesn't take long before he's talking about the people he's known and the things he's seen, with a sense of pride and passion. "Right after World War II was a magical era," he says. "There was a real sense of camaraderie that permeated the whole town of Petaluma. We had a profes-sional football team – the Leghorns. Fred "The Fox" Klemewok was the quarterback. They won 27 straight games and everybody in town came to see them play week after week."

In 1952, Torliatt joined the air force and spent the next five years in Japan, as an outsider. "I met a lot of interesting people when I wrote for *Stars and Stripes*," he says. "I also came face to face with the Japanese people. I learned about another culture. Most importantly, I married a Japanese woman. I think that my experience in Japan taught me to ask questions, not to hold on to old prejudices. When I came home, it didn't look the same."

In the late 1950s, Torliatt went to San Francisco State, and then to UC Berkeley where he earned an M.A. You might say he turned into a liberal. He's worked for the American Civil Liberties Union and he's supported the Catholic Worker, the long-standing organization of radical Catholics. He cares about the environment and race relations. These days, he gives rousing talks about local history to all sorts of people. He also swaps stories with local historians. "We have wonderful researchers and genealogists in Sonoma County," he says. "There are experts on sawmills, schools and railroads. There's so much change in the county. People want to hold on to the ways things were."

Part V:
Women Warriors

Dorothy Allison

Skin: Talking About Sex, Class & Literature

Over the past few decades, a growing body of innovative work – both fiction and non-fiction – has been written by, for and about lesbians. Much of it remains unknown to American readers at large, but some of it has spread beyond the lesbian subculture and reached a large and appreciative audience.

Dorothy Allison – who lives in Guerneville, not far from the Russian River – is one of the best known and most talented, as well as the sharpest, of the new lesbian literary stars. *Bastard Out of Carolina*, her first novel, was a National Book Award Finalist in 1992, and it made people sit up and take notice. Enthusiastically reviewed almost everywhere, it captures the world of poor white Southerners, and describes the devastating fall-out from domestic violence and sexual abuse in the "prison camp" of one nuclear family.

In *Trash*, a dazzling collection of short stories that appeared in 1988, Allison explored the unique contours of lesbian life. At the same time, she showed an extraordinary ability to make lesbian experience universal. Readers who listen carefully to her distinctive voice find that she speaks a language shared by many who have felt like outcasts and exiles in a culture that often demands unquestioned loyalty and conformity.

In *Skin*, a collection of two dozen essays written between 1981 and 1994 – many of them published in somewhat different form in *The New York Native* – Allison takes a close look at the connections between sex, class and literature, connections I wish my English teachers had made in college. All of the narrative essays were written in the first person, and in all of them Allison uses her own rich and varied life as a window to a larger, wider world.

As one might expect, the author writes about lesbians and feminists, about sexual desire and sexual abuse, and about pornography and popular fiction. "I am the wages of pulp," Allison writes in "Puritans, Perverts & Feminists," one of several insightful essays in which she talks about the books she has read and their influence on her own imagination.

To those who know little about the everyday lives of lesbians and who know even less about the complex politics of the lesbian community, *Skin* is as good an introduction as any that's available. In "Neighbors," for example, Allison explains that one of the things she liked best about living in New York was "the great number of queers," and that nobody looked twice at her as she walked down the street.

But this book isn't just about lesbians and lesbian issues. The fundamental themes here are poverty and privilege, fear and shame, and most of all telling lies and telling the truth. In "A Question of Class" – one of the longest as well as one of the most thought-provoking essays – Allison describes herself as "the bastard daughter of a white woman from a desperately poor family." For much of her life, she explains, she has had the urge to pack her bags, change her name, blend into the landscape and lie about her own past.

When she began to write, however, she made the crucial decision to claim her own family and her own history. She promised "to tell the truth not only about who I was but about the temptation to lie."

In "Sex Writing, the Importance and the Difficult" – which all writers, veterans as well as beginners, ought to read – Allison says that writing is "an attempt to sneak up on the truth" and that if "writing was dangerous, lying was deadly."

Some of the essays are repetitive, but Allison manages to come at her themes from different directions and now and then she changes the pace. In "Never Expected to Live Forever," which reads like a short story, she describes the time she sold beer and cigarettes at a drive-in store and was held up at gunpoint.

In "Promises," the last essay in the book, she describes the landscape of northern California where she lives now, and the emotionally charged landscape she knew as a girl growing up in Greenville, South Carolina. "The landscape of my imagination is all memory and passion, the wetland where I wandered as a child, the hidden places where I birthed my stories, widened my vision, plotted my escapes," she writes.

Skin shows that Allison is much more than the sum total of the pulp fiction that she's consumed for years. In fact, she's a serious intellectual and a profound social critic whose best essays belong with those of James Baldwin and Flannery O'Connor.

Dorothy Allison: "I'm Slowing Down as Fast as I Can."

"I'm 45 now," Allison says during an interview on a hot June afternoon at her home in Guerneville where she lives with her lover, Alix, and her son Wolf, who is nearly two and whom she calls "Junior."

"I don't write at the same pitch of anger that I did when I was writing *Trash*," she says. "I'm a mother now. I'm in a relationship with a woman I expect to be with for the rest of my life. I have three dogs and a garden. I'm slowing down as fast as I can."

But Allison doesn't seem to have slowed down at all. She has appeared at bookstores to autograph her work and to read from *Skin*, which she wrote for "feminist women in their forties and for my own sisters, who are not entirely feminist," she says.

Later, she'll teach at Hobart Smith College in upstate New York, and she'll travel to England in July to appear at a literary seminar on the American South, a place she knows very well.

"When I'm not changing diapers, cooking or writing, I'm reading," she says. "I read junk – the kinds of novels you get at airports. I'm hungry for fiction and there aren't enough books to read in the whole wide world."

Of course, Allison is also busy on a new novel called *Cavedweller*, which is "about three sisters who can't stand each other." Recently, she threw away 100 pages just like that. "Three-quarters of what you write is garbage," she says. "You have to learn to throw stuff away."

It sounds like a cliché, of course, but Dorothy Allison has come a long way since she was a young girl growing up poor in South Carolina. *Bastard Out of Carolina* was sold to Viacom, and that means that she doesn't have to worry about money for the first time in her life. But she has mixed feelings about material success.

"It made me nervous," she says. "It's scary, too. I've met legendary writers, and recently I was followed around all day by CBS-TV for a show they did about me. Suddenly I've got an enormous audience. It makes life a lot more complicated."

To get away from the fame and the stress, Allison retreats to an "outbuilding," as she calls it, so that she can concentrate on her writing. "When I'm in the middle of a book, I'm absolutely crazy," she says. "I become detached from reality. I'm afraid of interruptions, afraid I'll lose bits and pieces of the work. Sometimes I don't sleep for days."

While compiling the essays for *Skin*, Allison tried to complete an essay entitled "A Cure for Bitterness," which she hoped would help to close a chapter of her own life. But the door to that part of herself remains open. "I just couldn't finish it," she says regretfully. "I guess there's a level of bitterness I still need to work out."

In the privacy of her own home, Allison is quieter and shyer than I would have thought. But in a bookstore before an audience, she's stoked and she's outrageously funny. When she's on the road, her persona is fearless.

"I meet a lot of people who are wounded and who seem to need a hero, so I become heroic," she says. "I call my public persona "The All Purpose Mama.""

Gina Berriault

Women in Their Beds: New & Selected Stories

Gina Berriault – who was born in Long Beach, California over seventy years ago and who lives in Sausalito – has been writing and publishing spectacular short stories for more than half her life. After all these years, she has produced a large, innovative body of work that has brought her national acclaim. Indeed, no contemporary American author understands the unique properties of the short story better than Berriault, and no one has expanded the boundaries of the genre as far as she has.

In *Women in Their Beds,* which brings together 35 stories, some of them old, some of them new, all of them beautiful and haunting and mysterious, Berriault is at her very best, a writer who manages to be poignant, poetic, playful and very funny. You come away from these stories amazed that she has managed to reinvent a literary form that has been worked time and time again, and yet still remain true to a tradition of writers that includes Gogol, Hemingway, and Chekhov.

As the title of this volume implies, Berriault's stories are embedded in the realm of the sensual and the seductive. Indeed, they are often about romantic passion and sexual affairs. But in Berriault's world, beds are much, much more than simply playgrounds for men and women to seduce and be seduced, to love and be loved.

In "Women in Their Beds," for example, the very first story in this collection, a young social worker named Angela Anson goes to bed and makes love with a young San Francisco artist. But almost all of the other characters in the story – including a matriarchal, ninety-six-year-old gypsy queen – get into a series of hospital beds to rest, to sleep and to make their final departures from the world. In Berriault's stories, beds provide a space for solitude, sex, birth and procreation and death.

Without exception, the author never describes sexual encounters overtly, directly. And more often than not, she's concerned with the aftershocks of intimacy and the legacies of erotic couplings, not the lusts of the present moment. Thus, in "The Mistress," a young man meets an attractive older woman at an elegant party, unaware of the connection between them.

Taking the young man aside for a moment, the older woman explains that she and his father had an affair many years ago, a confession that leaves the son profoundly shaken. "You shouldn't have told me," he says, suddenly overcome by a sense of shame, and suddenly aware that he's not yet an adult.

Then, too, Berriault often describes men and women who seem as though they might become amorously involved, and yet never do. In "The Infinite Passion of Expectation" a 79-year-old psychologist waits for a young waitress, who is also his patient, to come to his bedroom, and when she fails to appear he pulls "back into himself his life's expectation."

Whether Berriault's subject is love, death, sexual betrayal or spiritual hunger, and whether she writes about aging academics, young musicians, or middle-aged artists and writers, her style is always sensual, always alluring. The language beguiles, arouses, caresses.

Reading the stories collected in *Women in Their Beds,* you feel catapulted into the midst of her characters' lives. Nothing is ever explained, and no one, neither the author herself nor any of her characters, offers a simple moral or anything remotely resembling a message. What we get instead are hints and clues, pieces in a complex puzzle we're invited to assemble.

In "Who Is It Can Tell Me Who I Am?" a highly literate homeless man makes the San Francisco library his home, then dies there. In "The Search for J. Kruper," a best-selling American novelist named Klipspringer goes to Mexico on a journey to interview the mysterious, reclusive author J. Kruper (a character inspired by the real life author B. Traven), only to be led on a wild-goose chase.

In "The Stone Boy," Arnold, a farm boy, kills his older brother Eugene, then goes into the field to pick peas, seemingly unaware that he's committed a crime, or done anything wrong. And in "Anna Lisa's Nose," a beautiful fashion model with a large nose leaves her loving husband Richard for a successful dentist with a big nose, then leaves the dentist for an Iranian named Muhammad who is unremarkable except that he has an immense nose, settling with him in Teheran, apparently to live happily ever after.

"Anna Lisa's Nose," "The Stone Boy," "The Search for J. Kruper," and "The Diary of K.W." are among the very best contemporary American short stories. They are stories you want to read and reread, stories that touch your heart, stories that bring you to the bedrock of love and loneliness, betrayal and joy.

Gina Berriault: Resisting the Critical Voice

Winning literary awards isn't new to Gina Berriault, who published her first novel in 1960, and her first collection of short stories in 1965. Years ago she received the Aga Khan Prize, the O. Henry Award and the Commonwealth Club Gold Medal. This year she has won more prestigious awards than ever before: the National Book Critics Circle and Pen/Faulkner Awards for fiction, and a $30,000 Rea Award for the Short Story. But so far, all these awards haven't made it any easier for Berriault to ply her craft.

"When I'm writing I work against the odds in my own head," she said during a recent phone conversation from her apartment in Sausalito. "I'm so critical of myself. All the time there's the feeling that it's not worthwhile, that it's nothing."

Born into a Jewish family in 1926, Gina Berriault grew up surrounded by adversity. Her father lost almost everything during the Depression of the 1930s, her mother went blind when Gina was still young, and her brother was regarded as demented by his teachers. "We were looked down upon by the neighbors," Berriault said. "We heard anti-Semitic remarks all the time. I was the skinny-legged kid, but I was the smartest in school."

Berriault's own experience seems to have provided her with a lifelong identification with outcasts and exiles, with "submerged people" who are "everywhere in our midst and who are looked down upon." Not surprisingly, her short stories are inhabited by characters who are lonely and lost. And not surprisingly, she writes about them "to stir sympathy for them."

From a very early age, Berriault began to write stories, and received encouragement from her father who wrote for trade publications. "He had a typewriter in his office," she said. "I'd watch him at work, and then I'd sit down and type. Because he was a writer I felt I could be one too."

Berriault's short stories have never come without intense labor. "I do a story over and over again," she said. "I do the first page over and over, and then I do the second page over and over. Then I do the whole story, and then I go back and redo the beginning, and then maybe the ending comes to me."

Still, she has happy memories of her life as a writer, especially in the 1960s and early 1970s when she and her daughter Julie Elena lived in Mill Valley, and Berriault sold her stories to *Esquire*. "We rented a house for $75 a month," she said. "You can't do that anymore. I'd get my daughter off to school, and then I'd write and when she came home we'd have supper, and then she'd go to bed, and I'd write until one or two in the morning."

Berriault taught at San Francisco State University in the late 1970s and early 1980s, and over the years she's made a respectable income writing for TV and for the movies.She's lived and worked in Massachusetts and in Iowa, but she always returns to northern California, a place she calls "my own turf." Berriault is working on two novels, hoping she'll finish one of them, but unwilling to say anything about either one of them for fear she'll lose them.

"I've never had a desire to be a public person and to go to parties and give readings," she said. "And I never anticipated winning awards. Now that I have them I don't know what to do about them, except that I need to go on writing, as I always have, in a sort of semi-reclusion."

Molly Giles

Creek Walk and Other Stories

If you're a guy and you're looking for guy fiction you won't find it in Molly Giles's *Creek Walk and Other Stories*, a collection of 14 short stories, most of them previously published in literary magazines over the past two decades, all of them elegantly crafted, and many of them about issues of disorder and control, of holding on and letting go.

Creek Walk is women's fiction. All the main characters are women – a librarian, a writer, a teacher of writing, to name just a few. They're not superwomen, wonderwomen or bigger-than-life Hollywood heroines – though in "The Blessed Among Us," which seems to be inspired by real-life local literary figures, there's a beautiful, best selling, Brazilian-born bombshell of a novelist named Iona.

Giles's women are middle class mothers, wives and daughters whom you might meet when you're shopping at the mall, exercising at the gym or waiting to see your therapist. They're profoundly troubled and deeply conflicted. And unlike the men in these stories, they're endowed with complex emotional lives, and caught up in the dilemmas of love and sex, life and death, work and family.

Creek Walk might also be called feminist fiction, though there's no sloganeering here, no waving of banners and no incitement to join a women's liberation group. Sisterhood isn't always powerful in Giles's stories, and men aren't always the natural predators of women. There are a few sensitive fellows sprinkled in these pages, but most of the male characters aren't exactly in touch with their feelings, and they aren't very good at communicating, either. You know men like this, and so do I.

They drink beer, watch TV and pursue women – sometimes harmlessly and sometimes with the explicit aim of assault as is the case in "Talking to Strangers," which is about a woman doctor who is brutally murdered. With the exception of this doctor, all the women in these stories are sturdy survivors. They may lose their jobs, grieve for deceased parents, and go through a divorce or two, but mostly they keep on going.

As you might expect, the blurbs on the dust jacket for the book proclaim Giles's extraordinary talent. "She is a virtuoso of the short story," Amy Tan writes. Lynn Freed exclaims, "Molly Giles is a world class writer."

Virtuoso for sure. Giles doesn't waste a word. Her stories are clearly focused, richly textured and her narrators always have distinctive voices. Giles is good at irony, sarcasm and satire. She shows, rather than merely tells, what happens, which is the advice that one of her characters gives her writing students.

Giles is talented, indeed, though to say she's world class may be a stretch. Read three or four of these stories and you have a good idea about the kinds of characters and scenes that will turn up in the next story. The style can be repetitive, too. The last sentence of a Molly Giles story is likely to be very long, and likely to tie up all the loose ends. At times, one wants to say to the author: Let it all unravel, lose control on the page. Experiment wildly!

Still, there are several stories here – "Leaving the Colonel," "Talking to Strangers," and "The Writer's Model" – which are exhilarating, shocking and truly memorable. The last story, "Untitled," which is about a teacher of creative writing and her students at a college that sounds like San Francisco State, but could be Sonoma State, ought to be required reading for anyone who has taught writing and for anyone who has ever taken a writing course in college.

I mean it! Buy this book. Read these stories. Maybe even some of you guys out there will find them entertaining or enlightening if only because you discover, strange as it may seem, that men aren't always at the center of the universe.

Molly Giles: Like Mother, Like Daughter

It's a Tuesday night and Molly Giles, who is the daughter of a writer and the mother of a writer, as well as a nationally acclaimed writer herself, is finally at home in Marin County after a long day at San Francisco State University, where she's a tenured professor and teaches classes in contemporary fiction and creative writing.

"I tell my students that writing can't be taught, but that it can be learned, and that they can get better with guidance and with practice,"

Giles says during a recent phone interview that takes place even as she's in the midst of making supper. If there are noises in the background, she explains, it's because she's cooking.

Born in California in 1942 to John and Doris Murphy, Molly grew up surrounded by books, in a family of strong women, and began to write poetry at age 7 or 8. Her own mother, whose first novel, *Cold Heaven,* was published in 1947, encouraged her to go on writing. "My mother read everything I wrote," she says. "She was very supportive."

After graduating from high school, she enrolled at the University of California at Berkeley, but dropped out at 19 to marry Daniel Giles, to have a family, and to raise three daughters – Gretchen, Rachael and Devon. At the age of 27 she went back to school – at Sacramento City College where she took English classes – and at 30 she signed up for a University of California extention course in creative writing. By that time her first marriage was coming apart, and she would soon be divorced, though she's kept his last name all these years.

It wasn't until 1978 that Giles finally received her B.A. from San Francisco State University. "It took me 18 years to finish my undergraduate education," she observes with a sense of pride. She goes on to say that, like a great many other women of her generation, her life has been defined by "unaccounted-for time" – long years that somehow can't be made to show up on a résumé.

Giles wrote poetry throughout her first marriage, and then again during her second marriage, but she never read it outloud, and never sent it off for publication. "I was a closet writer," she says. "I had no self-confidence."

The UC correspondence course helped her to believe in herself, and little by little she began to write fiction. "A story takes me a long, long time," she says. "Sometimes even a whole year. I rewrite and rework and rewrite again."

In 1985, the University of Georgia Press published *Rough Translations*, a collection of her short stories that was nominated for a Pulitzer Prize and that received the Flannery O'Connor Award for Short Fiction and the Bay Area Book Reviewer's Award for Fiction. Now she wasn't simply the daughter of a writer, but an accomplished writer herself.

Giles is also a celebrated writing teacher – her former students include Amy Tan, Gus Lee and Melba Beals, who are more famous than she is. Giles tells all her students that they need to trust themselves, and to believe that no one else can tell their own stories better than they can, a lesson she had to learn for herself.

Tonight, on the phone, she says she's just finished a draft of a novel that's about her mother, at least in part, that it's told in the third person, and that it's not ready to be sent out yet. "A novel is daunting," she says. "I find it very difficult to teach full time and to write an extended piece of fiction."

Meanwhile, *Creek Walk* is in the stores, and Giles is pleased. She's also proud of the fact that her oldest daughter Gretchen is a journalist, and that the family tradition of writing and publishing, which began with her mother has continued to the next generation. "I remember that as a child, Gretchen wanted to be a detective, and that she was also a great comic actress, but of course I'm delighted with her decision to become a writer."

Surely every mother would be.

Mavis Jukes

The Guy Book: An Owner's Manual

If I had to fix in time the golden age of my life as a guy, I'd say it began in 1955 when I turned 13 – and officially became a teenager – and ended in 1959 when I graduated from high school and went off to college to become a beatnik and a budding intellectual. Going back to college reunions has never really appealed to me, but I have long dreamed about going back to high school. In my senior year, I was the captain of the football team. I had a gorgeous cheerleader girlfriend named Charlotte and a car with a personality to match my own: a 1955 bright green British Morris Minor that stood out more than all those yellow buses in the school parking lot. And yet my years as a guy had many awkward moments. Much of the time I didn't know what was going on with my own body and what I might do about it. I didn't know the words "anxiety" and "alienation," but I was awfully anxious, and acutely alienated, too, and, as I later learned from high school reunions, many of the other guys felt the same way. Sometimes it was sheer agony to be a guy.

All of us would have benefited greatly from Mavis Jukes's *The Guy Book*, which is subtitled "An Owner's Manual." This compact book (152 pages) tells a guy almost everything he needs to know about how to live his life – and not run on empty – how to operate safely in the world, and how to maintain a sense of emotional well being. It is packed with information and there's information too about how to obtain even more information.

Of course, Mavis Jukes is not a guy. She's a mom – and a stepmom – with two independent-minded daughters, and she has written a lot of books about and for girls including *It's a Girl Thing: How to Stay Healthy, Safe, and in Charge* and *Growing Up: It's a Girl Thing*. I suppose it was inevitable that after writing guidebooks about how to grow up female, she would cross the great gender divide and write about growing up male. Maybe her efforts will help teenage guys and girls get together with understanding and even compassion for one another. That's a big part of her strategy.

Does Jukes know what it's really like for us guys? Is she qualified to write about the subject? Yes! Yes! She certainly knows what it's like for guys to grow up here and now at the start of the 21st century. It seems harder today than it was during my golden years as a guy in the mid-1950s. When I was in high school, we didn't have to worry about HIV, AIDS, drugs like LSD and ecstasy, and inappropriate sexual come-ons on the Internet. Sure, there were guys who identified with Liberace and not with James Dean and Elvis Presley, but it didn't seem as though there were that many different role models, and so much confusion about sex and gender. Life is more complex for all of us, and maybe especially for teenagers.

Jukes doesn't talk down to readers. She doesn't patronize, lecture, sermonize or scold. She plays the part of the concerned parent, the wiser older sister, and the coach who is always in your corner rooting for you. Her writing is informal, conversational and intimate, and she doesn't violate a guy's sense of privacy either. She tells it like it is – with a sense of respect. There's plenty of candid talk about sex – about the penis, testicles, sperm, erections, wet dreams, ejaculation and "solo sex." There's also lots of good news about love, passion and the libido. As a teenager I received scientific data from my teachers and from my dad, too, about male biology and male chemistry, but no adult ever said, as Jukes says, that sex can provide a sense of pleasure. I wish I'd heard that then.

Several chapters have an extra special section entitled the "The Guy Report" in which an anonymous guy or two talks about his own personal experiences – from shaving for the first time to that first nerve-racking high school dance. It's really cool to hear guys describe their experiences in their own words.

The information about manners is useful for almost any guy, whether he's 16 or 60. Jukes reminds us that teasing hurts, that belching probably won't make friends with, or find lovers among, members of the opposite sex. Random sexual remarks aren't nice and neither is staring at breasts. Are you guys listening? The practical advice is sound. It all makes sense, including the comments about self-confidence and self-respect. "What's in your head and what's in your heart are the most important things," Jukes writes. "In the long run, success is less about appearance – and more about performing life skills that you've developed like integrity, courage and compassion." I wish that a teacher or a guidance counselor had told me that in 1955 or 1956.

Will today's teenage guys turn away from their TVs, their cars, and their video games and take time to read this book? I hope so. The pictures of guys and their cars – of guys at the wheel and gorgeous girls next to them – certainly make this book enticing and a pleasure to look at. Jukes apparently feels that the way to a guy's heart and his head is through his car. Car talk, car pictures and the all-American metaphor of the car as a guy's sacred castle, mobile kingdom and extension of his personality run through this book, from beginning to end. We are what we drive, or so it's said, and Jukes takes full advantage of that notion to drive home her messages. Chapter 1 is entitled "Under the Hood: Parts," Chapter 7 is entitled "Sharing the Road: Girls," Chapter 9 is entitled "Parking: Sex." If you don't want to read from beginning to end, and want to use *The Guy Book* as a reference work, there's an excellent index that begins with abortion and acne and ends with wrestling and yoga. You can dive in to this book anywhere.

I recommend it for teenage boys, and the teenage boys in all men. I also recommend this book for parents and teachers, guidance counselors and therapists who work with teens. You may think you know everything there is to know about your own son, or the troubled kid in your class-room, or the culture of teenager boys. Maybe you do. But *The Guy Book* just might teach you a thing or two about date rape, unplanned pregnancy and sexual assault.

Mavis Jukes: From Tom Boy to California Girl to Guy Expert

Wouldn't you just know it! Mavis Jukes – the celebrated author of *The Guy Book* – comes from a family of proud women, strong women, inspiring women. Mavis's mother Marguerite taught hundreds if not thousands of students, and her sister Caroline grew up to become an influential school teacher, too. Of course, Mavis Jukes is a strong, proud, inspiring woman herself. Over the course of a lifetime – much of it lived in Sonoma County – she has been a mother, a wife, a school teacher, a homemaker, a homesteader, a role model and the author of 15 books, most of them for children and young adults.

And wouldn't you just know it, too! Mavis Jukes has been sur-rounded by strong men, proud men, inspiring men: her father Tom was a research scientist, her older brother Kenneth was an airplane pilot and her husband Robert Hudson is a nationally-acclaimed artist.

This morning Mavis Jukes is sitting at the dining room table of her Cotati home, where she lives with her husband and their dogs and cats. She's wearing jeans, sandals and a khaki work shirt – all of which a guy might wear – and her glasses sit atop her head.

"I was a part of the women's movement," she says. "In the old days, I might even have burned my bra if I hadn't had a real taste of power when I was a kid. I still consider myself a feminist. I also know that men and boys have their share of problems, too. I honor the struggles of men and boys."

Mavis Jukes was born just north of New York City and raised in Princeton, New Jersey where girls were supposed to behave like little women, and boys were supposed to behave like little men. "I was the total tom boy," she says. "I hung out with my older brother and his friends and learned how to build forts, change flat tires and use a hammer." Then, in her junior year of high school, Mavis moved with her family to El Cerrito, and after an initial culture shock to her whole system, she evolved into the complete California nature girl.

"I hooked up with guys who were mountaineer types," she says. "I wore Levis, sweatshirts and climbing shoes. I went backpacking with them in the wilds. I came of age in Yosemite." Then came higher education – at the University of Colorado at Boulder, and at the University of California at Berkeley. There she met Robert Hudson, her husband to be and the guy of her life – a painter, sculptor, teacher and ceramist whom she describes as a "Renaissance man." In the late 1960s and the early 1970s, she taught in Berkeley during the turbulent days of desegregation and busing. "That experience absolutely changed my life," she says. "I learned first hand the challenges that kids of color can have in a culture like ours that often discriminates. I was fortunate that African-American teachers like Dawson Boyd took me under their wing and made me real."

In the mid-1970s, Jukes attended Golden Gate Law School. She passed the bar exam on her first try, but something else seemed to be on her mind beside torts and contracts. When her husband Robert wondered why she didn't become an author instead of an attorney, she didn't have to think twice. She sat down at her desk and began to write books, not legal briefs. *No One Is Going to Nashville*, her first book, is about extended families. *Like Jake and Me*, a contemporary kid's classic, won the coveted Newberry Prize, and *Blackberries in the Dark*, which is about a young boy and his grandfather, is read in public schools from coast to coast.

While Jukes was writing books, she was also teaching, and learning about kids, too, from kids themselves. From 1995 to 1999, she taught art and the language arts in the Santa Rosa public school system – at Lincoln, Fremont, Hidden Valley, Proctor Terrace and Steele Lane. "I loved teaching in Santa Rosa," she says. "We did group projects about the law. We talked about violence and about media literacy. We looked at ads that were demeaning to teens, and we helped make kids aware of marketing and how to develop an intelligent approach."

If teaching in Berkeley in the 1960s changed Jukes's life, teaching in Santa Rosa in the 1990s changed it, too. For nearly a decade now, she has been on a mission to help teens get through their own troubles in these troubled times. Writing about teen girls came naturally. Writing about teen boys was a bit more of a challenge. "How can I write about guys?" she wondered. "I'm not a guy." Jukes received lots of encouragement from teenage boys in the Santa Rosa schools, and from their male teachers, counselors and principals – guys like Dino Ruffoni, George Viramontes, Steve Nielsen, Allan Yeager, John Huber, Ed Locker and Martin Forbes. They were a source of constant inspiration and invaluable information.

"One of the main things that I learned from writing *The Guy Book* is that the 'troubled parent/ teen relationship' is largely a myth that's been created by the media," Jukes says. "Most teenage boys are not surly, silent, crazy. They do not want to separate from their parents. They want to renegotiate their relationships. Our culture needs to give guys a break. Parents and teachers need to show kids that they're cared for and loved. Boys need nurturing, too."

Anne Lamott

Bird By Bird: Some Instructions on Writing and Life

Women have been writing, and writing about writing ever since writing was invented. But it's only been in the last decade or so that women writers have begun to give birth to a vast library of books about how, where and when to write, and most importantly, why one should write at all.

The recent birthing of books on the subject of writing began with Natalie Goldberg's *Writing Down the Bones*, which is now in its 19th edition. It was followed by Rita Mae Brown's *Starting from Scratch,* Deanna Metzger's *Writing for Your Life,* and Suzanne Lipsett's *Surviving a Writer's Life,* to name just a few of the many books that share the same shelf.

Anne Lamott, the Marin County novelist, restaurant critic and writing teacher, also offers her unique contribution to the subject in *Bird By Bird*. Like most of the books that precede it, Lamott's work is autobiographical, philosophical and literary – as well as a practical guide for would-be writers.

In *Bird By Bird*, we meet Lamott's father, who was a writer; her friends, many of whom are also writers; and the students who have attended her workshops and who seem to be more concerned with publication and fame than with the daily grind of writing itself.

Lamott – who was born in San Francisco and who lives in San Rafael – is almost always at the center of things, but for the most part she uses her own experience and her own emotional turmoil not to promote herself and her work but to help others find themselves.

Most of the advice makes perfect sense to me, and I've read passages from her book aloud to the Sonoma State University students who are enrolled in the writing class that I've been teaching for years.

"The very first thing I tell my students on the first day of a workshop is that good writing is about telling the truth," Lamott writes in the chapter entitled "Getting Started." These days I've been making much the same point in the classroom, and having those words from Lamott to back me up makes my job as a teacher a little bit easier.

Twice a month I get together with a group of men – a doctor from Petaluma, a rancher from Valley Ford, a businessman from Sebastopol, and a colleague from Sonoma State – to talk about our lives, to write for an hour or so, and to read our stories, poems and essays. *Bird By Bird* has a lot to say to all of us, too.

"You just have to keep getting out of your own way so that whatever it is that wants to be written can use you to write it," Lamott explains. In the chapter entitled "Giving," she writes, "You are going to have to give and give and give or there's no reason for you to be writing." Harsh words perhaps but true.

Lamott describes almost all of the occupational hazards she faces as a writer – jealousy, anxiety and insecurity – but she also manages to make fun of them and thereby surmount them. She's deadly serious and wildly funny at the same time.

Bird By Bird has sick jokes, entertaining anecdotes and words of wisdom. The chapter on plot, dialogue, character and setting are excellent for anyone who wants to write fiction. There's also a strong but very helpful section on libel and the 20-page introduction is a pure delight to read.

"What writing finally boils down to," Lamott says, "is putting down one damn word after another."

I guess it is. And I guess that's just what I've done right here and now.

Anne Lamott: Discovering Her Own Path

"The path that I was on would have led me to death," Anne Lamott said during a recent phone interview from Santa Monica were she was promoting *Bird By Bird*. "I was a very successful writer and I was famous, but with every book that I published I was more angry, more lonely and more depressed. I was dying of alcoholism. Eight years ago I got sober. Now I'm more alive. I'm a mother and a Christian and I'm loved by my friends. I tend to my soul, not to my ego and my reputation. I'm more concerned with being than with doing."

Lamott – who was born in 1954 and who studied philosophy and religion at Goucher College before dropping out after two years – says that she is not in therapy now but that she has benefited a great deal from therapy.

"I am a huge fan of therapy," she said. "Therapy helped me to throw off the backpack of who I was supposed to be and who my parents wanted me to become – and to find myself."

Writing has also helped her to discover her own identity. "Writing and therapy are both about who you are in this life," she said. "When you're sitting at the computer composing, you find a way to express yourself in your own voice."

The author of five books, including *Hard Laughter* (1980), *Rosie* (1983) and *Operating Instructions* (1993), she has been teaching writing workshops for a decade, mostly in northern California, and most recently at Book Passage in Corte Madera.

"Most of my students are women," she said. "Women know how therapeutic writing is, how fulfilling it can be. The women's movement showed us that with writing you could say what your life has been like. You could throw off all the revisionist history about childhood and marriage. You could tell the truth."

Lamott said that she thought that men might catch up one day and that they would join writing groups too. "Men haven't been that encouraged to dig around in their lives," she said. "That was supposed to be self-indulgent and 'womanly.' But writing will be a natural place for men to investigate their lives."

For years Lamott has also been in a reading group that includes several male members – Orville Schell, Ethan Canin and Adam Hochschild – all of them outstanding writers.

"We've reread many of the books that were required in college," she says. "But this time it's not to get the professor to love you more, but rather for the love of words and to be immersed in great works of fiction."

Introduction to Anne Lamott at Sebastopol Veterans Building
February 17, 1999

Her parents named her Anne Lamott, but everyone that I know calls her Annie, as though she were a big sister or a kid sister, or maybe an aunt or a cousin.

I don't know of any northern California writer who is more be-loved than Annie Lamott, and I don't know of any northern California writer who loves the land, the sea, the sky – the birds and the trees – of northern California more than she does.

If you have read Annie Lamott's books – and I'm sure that most of you have – I am probably not telling you something that you don't already know. But sometimes it helps to repeat the obvious.

I did not begin to read Annie Lamott until very recently and I have not seen her in person until this evening, though we did a telephone inter-view years ago when her book about writing, *Bird by Bird*, was first published. Somehow or other I knew from the moment I read the title that it wasn't going to be a book about ornithology. And I was right.

But I was pleasantly surprised when I read Annie Lamott's novels – *Rosie* and *Hard Laughter* and *All New People* and *Crooked Little Heart* – to find that they are inhabited by very real birds, all kinds of wonderful birds, birds with beaks and feathers – snowy white egrets and pelicans and gulls and mud hens and ducks, and owls and osprey and a redwing black-bird that I am especially fond of.

Sometimes Annie Lamott's birds fly freely – as freely as birds can fly – and sometimes they can be found in trees. And so, just as there are all kinds of birds in her books, there are all sorts of trees – both native and imported. There is eucalyptus, acacia, magnolia, fir, bay, buckeye, ash, sycamore, pine, pepperwood, oak, cypress, maple, elm, apple, plum and fig – the trees of northern California.

There is the smell of eucalyptus trees in *All New People*, and there are descriptions of ridges with "limitless trees" and hillsides that turn from green to golden yellow as early spring turns to late summer. And there are spectacular landscapes that are "as green as a rain forest."

But like the rest of us Annie Lamott has been watching the trans-formation of our northern California home, and so there are also descrip-tions of hillsides that are "covered with condominiums."

One of the things that's so wonderful about Annie Lamott's books is that she sees the trees, but she also sees the forests. She sees the tiniest, littlest growing things – the weeds that grow in the cracks of the sidewalk – and she also sees the big, big picture.

Annie Lamott is a writer who cares, a writer who belongs to the community and speaks for the community, even those communities in which there is "tyranny of public opinion."

She is also a very smart and a very funny writer. You can't help laughing – at least I can't – when she describes herself as a girl-child walking around "with my shoulders up to my ears," as she puts it and then adds "like Richard Nixon" – though I can't think of two people more dissimilar than Annie Lamott and Dick Nixon.

In *Bird By Bird*, Annie Lamott says that "Good writing is about telling the truth." To my way of thinking there is no more important job today than telling the truth about the earth, about the war on the earth that human beings are waging now and have waged for centuries, and about the possibilities for peace with the earth, on the earth.

In part, that's why we're here. And of course, we're here to hear Annie Lamott read from her new book, *Traveling Mercies: Some Thoughts on Faith*.

Alice Walker

The Same River Twice: Honoring the Difficult

Some years ago, when I was a Fulbright Professor in Belgium, I was invited to give a lecture at the American Cultural Center in Brussels on any contemporary American writer I wanted. Though I'd only read a handful of her books, and though I hadn't done exhaustive research about her, I decided I'd talk about Alice Walker, the Georgia-born author who has lived in northern California since the late 1970s, and who won the Pulitzer Prize for *The Color Purple*, (1982) her deeply spiritual novel about the love between black women in the South.

Ever since then I've continued to read everything that Walker has written – poetry, novels, essays and short stories – and most of the reviews and articles that have been written about her and her work. I've also stood back and watched as she's become an integral part of American literature – a required author in colleges and high schools and a cultural icon as well. Though Walker herself has rejected the role of role model, she has become an inspiration to women who refuse to shut up, or lie down quietly.

Walker is nobody's woman but her own. She has been making that message clear for years and she makes it again in her new book *The Same River Twice: Honoring the Difficult* which has a long and rather cumbersome subtitle, "A Meditation on Life, Spirit, Art, and the Making of the Film 'The Color Purple' Ten Years Later."

Recently when she spoke at the Mendocino High School commencement – which I attended – Walker told the graduating senior class, "Be pleased to walk alone," "Be an outcast," "Be nobody's darling," and "Take the contradictions of your life and wrap them around your life like a shawl."

The Same River Twice is Walker's homespun, patchwork shawl. It's her most confessional work and the riskiest she has yet written because it makes public her own inner contradictions, her anxieties, dreams and nightmares. Walker's own daughter Rebecca counseled her, she says, to "make this book very small and to publish it very quietly." Walker has chosen to do otherwise. Clearly she's felt it imperative to work out her own personal issues in a big book before a national audience, and with all the resources of a major publishing company.

The Same River Twice contains Walker's own screenplay for the film *The Color Purple*, her journal entries in which she talks about the movie, her letters to Steven Spielberg the director, and to Danny Glover the actor who played Albert in a role that outraged many black men. There are also previously published magazine interviews with and articles about Walker, and new essays by the author in which she talks candidly about her deceased mother, her intense mood swings and her own bisexuality, which many readers of *The Color Purple* have long suspected.

Those who like to peer into the private lives of celebrities may find portions of this book enticing. Walker describes the black silk dress with sequins and gold leaves that she wore to the premiere for *The Color Purple*. She muses about Steven Spielberg's astrological sign – he's a Sagittarius – and her own sign – she's an Aquarius, and she describes herself as a "born-again pagan."

Walker, however, does not pander to voyeurs or appeal to prurient interests. *The Same River Twice* is a serious and an important work in the on-going story of Walker's struggle to understand sex, race, class – and to heal her own emotional and psychological wounds.

Moreover it's an invaluable sourcebook for students of Walker's work and a fascinating account of what happens when a creative writer becomes caught up in Hollywood. What emerges in these pages is a woman who is torn between personal values and political commitments. So, for example, Walker explains that when she was on the set of *The Color Purple* she refused Stephen Spielberg's request that she appear in a scene holding his newborn son Max.

"I could not," she writes in an emotional letter to the director. "There is just too much history for that to have been possible. It's a very long Southern/South African tradition, after all – black women holding white babies. And yet I felt so sad for all of us, that this should be so."

Walker finds herself admiring Spielberg, though he knows almost nothing about her own culture and heritage, and though he insists that *Gone with the Wind* is the greatest movie ever made, a perspective that infuriates her. Moreover, she tries awfully hard to like Spielberg's cinematic version of her novel and hates to admit that it "looks slick, sanitized and apolitical."

In one of the most moving sections of the book, Walker describes her troubled feelings about her own mother, a black woman who began life as a sharecropper in Georgia, and thus might appear as a heroic figure of resistance to oppression. But the author is disturbed by her mother's anti-Semitism as well as her prejudice against lesbians, and her Christian fundamentalism.

Walker's honesty is admirable. I found myself appreciating her willingness to explore her own divided self – to wear the shawl of her own contradictions in public. Still I would have liked this book to have been more polished and more analytical. I wish Walker had taken the opportunity to draw more explicit and more direct links between her own experience and the life of our culture and the nation as a whole. *The Same River Twice* contains so much – there are thoughts and comments about O.J. Simpson, apartheid in South Africa, homosexuality, black music, television and civil rights, to name just a few – that there isn't a great deal of time to discuss important subjects in depth.

If you haven't read Walker and don't know her work, I'd recommend that you start with the short stories collection, *In Love & Trouble*, or her first novel, *Meridian,* which describes the civil rights movement of the 1960s. But if you already know and love her books, especially *The Color Purple* and *Possesssing the Secret of Joy,* then by all means read *The Same River Twice*. You'll see Walker behind the scenes – coming to terms with her own past and remaking her identity.

Anything We Love Can Be Saved: A Writer's Activism

June 11, 1997
Dear Alice Walker:

Have you ever thought about the titles of your books and how they suggest the fundamental life-changes you've been through? In the beginning there was *The Third Life of Grange Copeland, In Love and Trouble,* and *Revolutionary Petunias,* all of which suggest a certain playfulness and an air of mystery. Then came *The Color Purple* and *In Search of Our Mothers' Gardens*, which suggest exploration and transcendence.

More recently your books have had titles that offer simple declarative statements and sometimes sound like slogans. There's *Horses Make a Landscape Look More Beautiful* and *The Same River Twice: Honoring the Difficult*. Now there's *Anything We Love Can Be Saved*. The idea is thought provoking, but I don't believe it's true. Indeed, there are things we love that probably can't be saved, no matter how hard we try.

The title of your new book isn't the only thing that troubles me. Reading some of the essays, I heard myself say, "What world are you living in? Wake up, Alice Walker! Get real!"

Then, before I finished the book, I went to hear you (and the Dalai Lama, among others) at the Peacemaking Conference in San Francisco, and I came to see you in a new way. You seemed so down-to-earth, so present and so willing to listen to people. At the workshop that you gave, I was struck by the fact that you've become a cultural icon of political correctness and that your readers expect you to speak out against injustice and insensitivity – and support every good cause on the face of the earth. I also realized, for the first time, that you have a sense of humor. Hearing you read the essay "The Universe Responds," in which you write about George, the freedom-loving, Mendocino County dog who shows up at your doorstep, I broke out in laughter. After the conference I went back to the book and finished it with a more receptive state of mind. I'm writing you now to tell you that what I like most about *Anything We Love Can Be Saved* is your candor. I was moved by your willingness to tell readers that in the 1960s you felt resentment toward white people who, like you, were active in the civil rights movement. And I appreciate your willingness to write that people who want to change the world are often deeply flawed individuals. Young people today need to know that they don't have to be perfect to want to make a more perfect world, that imperfection is part of being human, and that everyone we love is imperfect.

Sometimes I wish you'd go more deeply into a subject. When you say that you're happier now in northern California than any other place you've lived, I wanted to know why. Sometimes you seem to skim over the surface – as in your essays on the psychologist Carl Jung and the poet Audre Lord. And sometimes you don't explain how you reach a conclusion. For example, you say that "the dominant culture is designed to encourage the full development of the white and the male only, and not even of the disadvantaged in those categories."

Most of the wealthy, powerful white men I've met hardly qualify as fully developed individuals, either emotionally or intellectually. You also say, "What is happening more and more in the world is that people are attempting to decolonize their spirits." Some people seem to be engaged in that process, but I've also noticed a lot of people killing their spirits with drugs, sex and violence.

At the Peacemaking Conference you read from your early novel, *Meridian,* which you described as a spiritual autobiography. Listening to you, it occurred to me that in the past decade or so, as you've become an international advocate for the incarcerated and the afflicted, your writing has lost some of the richness and complexity I found in *The Third Life of Grange Copeland, Meridian* and *The Color Purple*. As you've taken on issues like female genital mutilation, and as you've made large numbers of readers around the world aware of crucial social problems, you've written books that haven't explored the human predicament as deeply or as fully as you once did. My plea to you is to write more books – at least some of the time – that go beyond slogans and causes. Let your imagination go.

I know there is no going back, and no sense trying to repeat yourself. The only thing to do is to keep writing and to continue to remain true to yourself. I'll go on reading you because, though you're a black woman and I'm a white man – though we're very different individuals – I've learned a lot from your writing about sensuality, politics and art.

At the Peacemaking Conference you said, "At some point you must take your bleeding heart and look at the blue sky from the side of the hill." I like that image and that thought. Alice, you've been on the side of a hill in Mendocino. I've been on the side of a hill in Sonoma. The same blue sky arches above us, as it arches above so many others with wounded hearts on so many hillsides all over the earth.

Sincerely,
Jonah Raskin

Appendix

Selected Books by Northern California Writers

Now that you've read about California writers and their work you might want to read the writers themselves. There are too many books by too many authors to list them all – without making an appendix that would be longer than this book itself. I have picked out some books that I've enjoyed. The books listed here seem to me to represent the author at his or her best – or else they capture an essential quality of northern California. There is an emphasis here on Sonoma County writers, though there are also writers from Marin, Napa, Mendocino, and Humboldt counties. I hope you enjoy reading our literature. If you belong to a reader's group, and you'd like me to come and talk, please email me at jonah.raskin@sonoma.edu and I will be in touch.

Aaron, Chester. *Garlic is Life*
Allende, Isabel. *House of the Spirits*
Allison, Dorothy. *Bastard Out of Carolina*
Anderson, Robert Mailer. *Boonville*
Andrews, Sarah. *Mother Nature*
Baer, Barbara. ed. *Saltwater, Sweetwater*
Barich, Bill. *Carson Valley*
Beeman, Robin. *A Minus Tide*
Berriault, Gina. *Women in Their Beds*
Boldt, Brian. *One Never Knows Do One?*
Brautigan, Ianthe. *You Can't Catch Death*
Brennan, Kevin. *Parts Unknown*
Bromige, David. *Desire*
Brown, Carrie. *The Jimtown Store Cookbook*
Carlson, Elizabeth. *Collected Poems*
Chadwick, Cydney. *Enemy Clothing*
Chiarello, Michael. *Napa Stories*
Conoley, Gillian. *Lovers in the Used World*
Cook, Carolyn. *The Bostons*
Cook, Laurel. *Spas of California*
Coshnear, Daniel. *Jobs and Other Preoccupations*
Di Prima, Diane. *Loba*

_____. *Grand Ambition*
McCarroll, Tolbert. *Thinking with the Heart*
McDonald, Megan. *Judy Moody*
McMains, Victoria. *The Reader's Choice*
Montroy, Pierrette. *Gratitudes*
Moody, Bill. *Looking for Chet Baker*
Muller, Marcia. *Dead Midnight*
Oxenhandler, Noelle. *The Eros of Parenting*
Packer, Ann. *The Dive from Clausen's Pier*
Parvin, Roy. *In the Snow Forest*
Perkins, Fiona. *The Horse Orchard*
Pronzini, Bill. *A Wasteland of Strangers*
Raphael, Ray. *An Everyday History of Somewhere*
Rasberry, Salli & Carol Wantanabe. *The Art of Dying*
Rathmell, George. *Realms of Gold*
Rosen, Gerald. *The Carmen Miranda Memorial Flagpole*
Rubin, Charles. *4-F Blues*
Sarris, Greg. *Grand Avenue*
_____. *Watermelon Nights*
Saxton, Alexander. *Bright Web in the Darkness*
Sloat, Teri. *Dance on a Sealskin*
Snyder, Gary. *The Gary Snyder Reader*
Solnit, Rebecca. *Wanderlust*
Sterling, Joy. *A Cultivated Life*
Stone, Sarah. *True Sources of the Nile*
Stout, Doug. *Sometimes I'm Surprised*
Swartz, Susan. *Juicy Tomatoes*
Tan, Amy. *The Joy Luck Club*
Torliatt, Lee. *Golden Memories of the Redwood Empire*
Walker, Alice. *The Same River Twice: Honoring the Difficult*
_____. *The Temple of My Familiar*
Wendt, Chip. *Cold Valley Poems*
Whitty, Julia. *A Tortoise for the Queen of Tonga*
Wilson, J. J. and Karen Petersen. *Women Artists*
Wilson, Simone. *The Russian River*

Index

A

Aaron, Chester 4, 161
Alexander Valley 61, 62
Allende, Isabel 5, 54-57,116, 161
Allison, Dorothy 6, 131-134, 161
Andrews, Sarah 95-98, 161
Anything We Love Can Be Saved 155, 156

B

Baer, Barbara 6, 161
Baker, Chet 99-102, 162
Barich, Bill 5, 59-62, 161
Bastard Out of Carolina 6, 131, 133, 161
Beats 12, 13, 18, 20, 22, 23, 40, 115
Beeman, Robin 5, 49, 69-71, 161
Berriault, Gina 135-138, 161
Big Dreams 59
Bird By Bird 148-152
Bonesetter's Daughter 63-68
Bono, Susan 6
Bright Web in the Darkness 72-74, 163

C

Call of the Wild 11-14
Camp Meeker 71
Can Poetry Matter? 3, 162
Carson Valley 59-62, 161
Cazadero 25
Chandler, Raymond 95, 108
Chiarello, Michael 76-80, 161
Clare, Carolina 6
Color Purple 153-155, 157
Coming of Age in California 36, 37, 162

About the Author

Jonah Raskin has lived and worked in northern California since 1975. He is the chairman of the communication studies department at Sonoma State University, and the author of several books: *Out of the Whale*; *My Search for B. Traven*; *For the Hell of It: The Life and Times of Abbie Hoffman;* and *More Poems, Better Poems*. His book reviews and profiles of authors appear regularly in *The Press Democrat* and his radio program "Walks of Life" can be heard on KRCB.